Series / Number 02-022

Linguistic Analysis of Political Elites: A Theory of Verbal Kinesics

ROBERT SHELBY FRANK
The Foreign Policy Research Institute

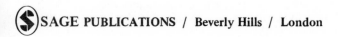 SAGE PUBLICATIONS / Beverly Hills / London

For information address:

SAGE PUBLICATIONS, INC.
275 South Beverly Drive
Beverly Hills, California 90212

SAGE PUBLICATIONS LTD
St George's House / 44 Hatton Garden
London EC1N 8ER

International Standard Book Number 0-8039-0360-X

Library of Congress Catalog Card No. 73-92216

FIRST PRINTING

When citing a professional paper, please use the proper form. Remember to cite the
correct Sage Professional Paper series title and include the paper number. One of the
two following formats can be adapted (depending on the style manual used):

(1) AZAR, E. E. (1972) "International Events Interaction Analysis." Sage Professional Papers in International Studies, 1, 02-001. Beverly Hills and London: Sage
Pubns.

OR

(2) Azar, Edward E. 1972. *International Events Interaction Analysis.* Sage Professional Papers in International Studies, vol. 1, series no. 02-001. Beverly Hills and
London: Sage Publications.

CONTENTS

Linguistic Analysis of Political Elites: A Theory of Verbal Kinesics

ROBERT SHELBY FRANK
The Foreign Policy Research Institute

INTRODUCTION

International studies as an intellectual endeavor is beginning to reassert the importance of national and international elites as causal agents of international behavior. The "real world" accomplishments of the Kissingers of the world, whether for good or for bad, again are highlighting the importance of political-elite analysis. Without getting into the long-standing "level-of-analysis" problem (see Singer, 1968a), we agree with Kelman (1965: 587) that the study of political elites can be justified only if it can be shown that the individual is "a relevant unit of analysis for the study of international politics."

In spite of the enormous amount of scholarly ink that has been devoted to elite analysis and in spite of the amount of intellectual heat generated by protagonists in the level-of-analysis issue, no definitive research is available to date that maps out the relative weight of macro versus micro explanations of international behavior. One interesting formulation would be to consider macro-political, social, and economic variables as necessary but not sufficient background agents upon which and within which various national and international elites interact. In the final analysis, however,

AUTHOR'S NOTE: *I wish to gratefully acknowledge the kind and insightful assistance of Margaret Hermann, who read and made extensive comments of earlier drafts of this paper. To Vincent Davis, whose patience and intellectual encouragement made this paper possible, a special debt of gratitude is owed.*

this author accepts the formulation of Allport (1950: 43) as applied not only to war but also to significant international behaviors in general:

> The people of the world—the common people themselves—never make war. They are led into war, they fight wars, and they suffer the consequences; but they do not actually make war. Hence, when we say that "wars begin in the minds of men" we can mean only that *under certain circumstances leaders can provoke and organize the people of a nation to fight.* Left alone people themselves could not make war.

Elite analysis is of central importance to the field of international studies. For scholars who have tackled this field of elite analysis, the strategies of explanation as well as the roles assigned to the elites in the general political process are varied. A few examples will suffice. There are scholars who propose a role for elites or "decision makers" within a tri-partite or quadri-partite model that generally includes as a minimum the decision maker, the decision-making context (e.g., crisis), and the respective political structures in which the decision-making is conducted (Snyder, Bruck, and Sapin, 1962; Farrell, 1966). Others accept this basic framework and attempt to show how changing contexts create different modes of decision-making in the decision makers themselves (Holsti, 1965; Verba, 1961; Zinnes, 1968; C. Hermann, 1969; Greenstein, 1969: 51-57). Still others use a somewhat "reverse" strategy of measuring political values of various elites, ascertaining which of these values have been politically realized, and then inferring which groups from the subnational level "have power" in a macro-level context (Deutsch and Edinger, 1959; Jensen, 1966). Of those scholars who impute any causal role to elite actions in international affairs, the assigned roles range from a secondary intervening variable (Coplin, 1971: 27; Wilkinson, 1969: 115) through elite importance when elite goals correspond to goals of the "chief lieutenants" and the "populace" (North, 1968: 342-343) to assertions that (at least in the making of foreign policy) for at least one country (the United States) national action is determined solely by one individual (the President) or, if he abrogates his duties in this field, then it is left to the vagaries of "fate" (de Rivera, 1968: 105).

Whatever the actual weight and the role-in-political-process occupied by national and international elites, this paper simply accepts as axiomatic that such elites are important and that they deserve more complete and more sophisticated analysis. This study looks at the verbal communication of one subset of political elites, i.e., presidents of the United States. Such verbal communication constitutes an important component of the overall political process in two very distinct fashions. On the one hand, the language of politics from elite to mass, especially the flow of political symbols, impacts directly at the macro-political level. The failure of elites to use "proper" symbols during communication can lead to system instability and lack of cohesion (Blau, 1964: 199-223), internal conflict and structural strain (Smelser, 1962: 51-56; Geertz, 1964, 1967), continuations of outmoded forms of social consensus (Pool, 1970: 9), and failures to maximize political power (Janos, 1964: 133; Sullivan, 1972: 190; Snyder, 1961).

On the other hand, elite communication can serve as an "indicator of personal psychological attributes and/or states." Certain scholars such as Donley and Winter (1970) code "need power" statements as representing the actual needs or desires for power in the communicator. In such a research strategy, there is assumed to exist a one-to-one semantic correspondence between what is psychologically "felt" and what is verbally communicated.

Others scholars infer latent psychological or psychopolitical states and/or traits from that which is communicated without making the assumption of one-to-one semantic equivalence. As Brown (1958: 308) notes: "Some linguistic categories are treated as signs of their referent categories but will not be used as names of them; we shall call these *symptoms.* A tremulous voice may be symptomatic of fear in the speaker but it is not the name of fear." The present study accepts this second approach and, as will be argued more fully later in this paper, accepts the notion that only through the use of this "symptomatic approach" can international studies scholars utilize cross-national, cross-cultural, and cross-linguistic "semantic equivalencies" for the comparative study of political elites. The search for cross-national semantic as well as behavioral equivalencies *is* the key obstacle in the path to comparative elite analysis (Merritt, 1970; Przeworski and Teune, 1970; Hymes, 1970).[1]

To sum up to this point, we have argued that elites can be analyzed by examining their communication output, either directly through assuming that they mean what they say and they say what they feel, or, indirectly through establishing a series of semantic transformation rules[2] to interpret the meaning behind the communication. It also has been argued that elites are important not only as decision makers but also as elite-to-mass communicators as is portrayed in Figure 1.

Such a model does not, of course, explore all the ramifications of elite-mass-national behavior interactions. The aggregation of demands and supports (Easton, 1965; Almond and Powell, 1966) must be more fully explored. A major compendium of articles dealing with sources of national

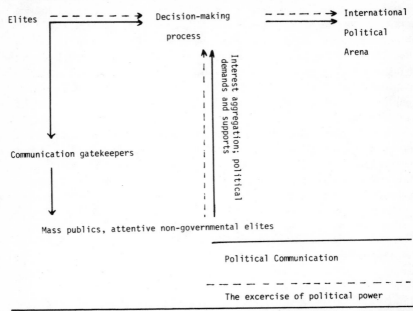

Figure 1: A TWO-DIRECTIONAL MODEL OF THE MACRO-LEVEL IMPACT OF ELITE BEHAVIOR

behavior, for example, goes no further than studying the ways in which elites and mass publics mutually evaluate each other (Singer, 1965: 231-326). Another series of intellectual problems revolves around the problem of "mediating interpreters of communication," i.e., the gate-keepers and their peer-group function of "interpreting" externally generated communication (Lerner, 1958; Katz, 1957; Pool, 1963; Lerner, 1963; and in general, Pye, 1963).

Elites, therefore, have a dual function in national and international relations. Presidents of the United States obviously rank among the most important members of this cluster of political actors. Through the utilization of the techniques described later in this paper, both the policy maker and the scholar will be presented with an analytical tool for measuring levels of psychopolitical stress as manifested in the communication of such elites. These techniques, based upon indicators that are neither linguistically nor culturally bound, easily can be extrapolated to the comparative analysis of non-American elites. Knowledge of the areas of personal concern for a given decision maker is of course important not only in anticipating those issue areas that the policy maker does now and will in the future consider to be salient and important; knowledge of such stressed issue areas can predict styles of political behavior when that issue is finally confronted.[3]

One of the central responsibilities of leadership or elite analysis is the presentation of a model by which elite behavior can be studied and explained. The number of psychological models that political scientists have adopted and the number of hybrid explanations that they have generated are certainly much too numerous for anything more than a brief overview here. Certain major schools of thought can be identified. Davies (1963) and more recently Knutson (1972) and Renshon (1972) have attempted to explain political behavior in terms of meeting a hierarchy of personal needs. In large part these political scientists have drawn upon the need-gratification theories of Murray (1938; 1951), Kluckhohn, Murray, and Schneider (1953), and especially Maslow (1954).

There are some major problems with this approach, some of which are lucidly reviewed by Lane (1969: 21ff). Perhaps the most challenging problems for those who wish to use this framework include the operational specification of the needs that the individual attempts to satisfy and the problem of ascertaining the relationships between "utility curves" and schedules for simultaneously meeting various needs.[4]

Another approach has been to rely heavily upon psychoanalytic theory that is then applied to the examination of individual political elites (George and George, 1964; Glad, 1966; Edinger, 1965; Erikson, 1958 and 1969; Freud and Bullitt, 1967; Rogow, 1963; Lifton, 1968; Merritt, 1965).[5] Unfortunately, the intuitiveness and the lack of formal motivational explication of this type of study seriously compromises the intellectual worth of this line of analysis.[6] The most rewarding of these types of studies generally tends to be those psychobiographies that rely least heavily upon classical Freudian explanation (Marsh, 1971; Wills, 1969). Such studies can produce insights not only into the subject investigated but also into the workings of the political mind. Nevertheless, it seems unlikely that any formalized and empirical framework will be forthcoming from this strategy of explanation.

A more profitable approach seems to be the development of typologies of political personalities based upon a specific psychological phenomenon or upon the interaction of a limited series of motivating factors. Harold Lasswell (1960, original 1930; 1962, original 1948; 1935 and 1968) exemplifies this first approach with his theory of personal displacement into the political arena. James David Barber is representative of the second approach, i.e., that of combining a small number of psychopolitical dimensions. Barber's "activity" and "willingness to return" dimensions and his "active-passive" "positive-negative" framework (1972) are solid theoretical starting points, although Barber's lack of empirical investigation detracts from the value of his work.[7] The strength of Barber's (1972) study of American presidents lies in the fact that he clearly presents a model that is highly compatible with traditional learning theory approaches from psychology. Moreover, his five supplementary concepts of "character," "world view," "style," "power situations," and "climate of expectations" constitute an interesting series of intervening variables that should increase the explanatory power of his theory. Other notions of career expectations (p. 99), historical identity and the flowering of political virtue (p. 449), and the role of the need to "control" oneself and one's undifferentiated psychic energy (pp. 99ff). (See also Barber's statement: "All of this left a lot of emotional energy in search of someplace to go," [p. 105] as an example of the almost Hullian drive-model of motivation.) These and other introjections may add to the richness of Barber's model, although at present their place in his scheme is somewhat unclear.

A fourth strategy of leadership analysis and one which has not produced the quantity of studies as have the first three orientations is exemplified by Herman Finer's (1964) study of Dulles' role in the Suez Crisis of 1956. Unlike the psychoanalytic approach, which draws from the historical record in an attempt to convince the reader of the importance of the given psychoanalytic framework, Finer presents a closely researched and reported chronology of the historical events for a limited period of time and shows how, at various stages of the crisis, the psychological characteristics of Dulles impacted upon the development and the resolution of the crisis. Identifying basically the same important personality characteristics of Dulles that Holsti (1962) worked with, Finer's study is a superior example of how the historical record and a psychodynamic approach can be given equal weight in the explanation of a chronology of events.

A fifth approach can be characterized as treating the elite as an "information-processing" device complete with inner circuits and memory banks and subject to its own internal gatekeeping devices. At the most general level of abstraction, this approach is very compatible with the assumptions underlying the various content analytic studies and simulation programs that have been applied to the outbreak of World War I. We include in this fifth category, however, those scholars who have attempted to develop a formal schematic explanation for the processing of political stimuli (Deutsch, 1963; Tolman, 1951; Smith, 1968).

Finally, reference should be made to the variations of the frustration-aggression approach in explaining the political behavior of individuals. The studies that explicitly or implicitly embrace this formulation are far too numerous to mention. Perhaps Gurr's (1970) reformulation of this approach in terms of "relative deprivation" is the most ambitious formalized attempt to work with this basic frustration-aggression paradigm. Such a formulation, however, is in itself inadequate to explain even political aggression. Davies "J-Curve" model (1962) and Schwartz' notion of personal and systemic efficacy (1970) are welcome revisions of the basic frustration-aggression model. Whether or not these additions can "save the theory" is as yet empirically undetermined.

Each of these six general ways of explaining political behavior has its strengths and weaknesses. Even psychoanalytic descriptions of behavior, perhaps the most suspect form of explanation of those listed above, serves the function of reminding us that in the last analysis, the notion of psychic drives must be taken into account. Hilgard and Bower (1966: 271-273; originally 1948) note that especially the Freudian treatment of "anxiety" has contributed to more behavioral treatments of learning and motivation.

The present study, however, takes a somewhat different approach to the study of personality and motivation. In short, this study employs a model built around a three-dimensional response-mode analysis that relies heavily upon state instead of trait analysis and that posits a major role to situational variables as accounting for the specificity of individual behavior.

Most of the strategies of explanation discussed above that have been adopted by political scientists invariably contain a categorization of individuals by personality traits or combination of traits, or posit a simple unidimensional stimulus-response chain (the frustration-aggression hypothesis). These traits or behavior chains are seen as highly generalizable and stable across a wide range of the elite's behavior. Actors are seen as "nationalistic," "dogmatic," "active (or passive)," or as exhibiting any number of personality traits irrespective of situational pressures.

Unfortunately, the empirical evidence to support these trait constructs is often rather weak and/or ambiguous.[8] Moreover, the very specificity of situational constructs in terms of personality testing situations in large part accounts for the lack of empirical verification of enduring and stable personality traits across a variety of situations.[9] The arguments against the description of personality and human behavior in terms of a trait analysis model have been thoroughly reviewed by Mischel (1968). After reviewing major attempts at trait validation, Mischel concludes:

[I] t is evident that the behaviors which are often construed as stable personality trait indicators are actually highly specific and depend upon the details of the evoking situations and the response mode employed to measure them [p. 37].

With the possible exception of intelligence, highly generalized behavioral consistencies have not been demonstrated, and the concept of personality traits as broad response predispositions is thus untenable [p. 146].

Toward the end of his review of the efforts to determine or to identify the presence of personality traits, Mischel writes:

Although behavior patterns often may be stable, they usually are not highly generalized across situations.... [B]ehaviors depend upon highly specific events but remain stable when the consequences to which they lead and the evoking conditions remain similar [p. 282].

Most prediction studies of personality have been guided by trait and state theory with the assumptions that behavioral signs can reveal enduring generalized personality structures that serve as broad behavioral predispositions, and that future behavior is chiefly determined by these predispositions. These two basic assumptions focus on stable individual difference or personality variables as the key determinants of behavior; they largely ignore the role of environmental conditions or stimulus situations in the regulation of behavior. As has been stressed repeatedly, however, individuals discriminate sharply among even seemingly close stimulus situations and consequently the widespread response consistencies assumed by trait theories usually do not exist [p. 293].

Mischel does not totally reject trait analysis. He notes the endurance of generalized stabilities especially in terms of personal definitions of the self and in terms of social definitions of the individual's role. These he calls "constructed stabilities" (pp. 284-285) and admits to their role in determining individual behavior.[10] Moreover, Mischel admits to the probability of at least one highly predictive trait, i.e., intelligence. Nevertheless, Mischel presents convincing arguments that compel the development of a model of behavior that is more sophisticated than the trait analysis generally accepted in political science and in elite psycho-political analysis.[11]

Others have worked with a series of trait variables while admitting the importance of situational determinants as a predictor to behavior. Lazarus (1966) attempts to utilize the notions of "anxiety proneness" and "social sophistication" as partial explanations of reaction to threat, yet his exhaustive treatment of "secondary appraisal" as a predictor to coping routines relies heavily upon the characteristics of the threatening situation and upon the cognitive evaluation of the situation by the stressee (pp.

150-257). Behavioral responses, according to Lazarus, can be radically different according to the subject's evaluation of the threatening situation.

Greenstein (1969: 13), while arguing for "deep" personality dimensions[12] argues for taking into account the situations in which behavior is evoked:

> It has often been said that there is no "one-to-one correlation" between psychological dispositions and action. It is not as often appreciated that the correlation can even be *negative;* in some circumstances, an individual's behavior may actually be the reverse of what would have been expected if merely his predispositions were taken into account [pp. 125-126].

Greenstein (p. 98) notes the problems of discriminating between political and psychological responses, and he concludes his book on politics and personality with this admonition:

> Accounts of the phenomenology of a political actor—of the regularities in the ways in which he presents himself to the observer—are the most immediately relevant supplement to situational data in predicting and explaining the actor's behavior. And these accounts, if they stay close enough to the texture of the observables, can be agreed upon by investigators with theoretical interests as diverse as learning-theory and psychoanalysis. The constructs used to characterize psychological dynamics—the inner trends accounting for the outer regularities—are more difficult to agree upon and are less immediately necessary for analyses of behavior. By and large, explanations of genesis pose even more difficult questions of validation, and these are most remote from the immediate nexus of behavior [pp. 144-146].

This discussion of the strategy of explanation of human behavior attempts to emphasize the following points:

(1) Political scientists have looked to a number of explanations of human behavior ranging from case studies to personality types and from psychodynamics to a more restricted and formalized interaction of personality traits.

(2) In addition to theoretical weaknesses unique to each of these explanations, these approaches for the most part have ignored the importance of stimulus conditions and of behavioral response states.

(3) State analysis is suggested by the the relative weakness of trait theories to stand the empirical tests of stability and situational generalizability.

(4) Furthermore, state analysis investigates what Greenstein has called the "observables" of behavior, observables that are not removed from "the nexus of behavior" and that do not suffer as greatly from the problems of validation that have haunted trait-centered explanations.

The foregoing statements do not mean that this writer necessarily rejects the place of inner drives, needs, and personality traits as eventually contributing to the full understanding of elite behavior. It is suggested, however, that state analysis and personal variation along with a limited series of state dimensions (1) can tell us quite a bit about psychopolitical response to specific situations and (2) can be more readily identified and agreed upon as important behavioral responses in the prediction of elite behavior.

In spite of Mischel's admonitions, a number of trait theories have at least the potential to contribute eventually to psychopolitical explanation. Eysenck's introversion-extroversion dimension (1957, 1967), based upon physiological differences among subjects is promising, as is Witkin's formulation of personality differences as a function of perceptual abilities (1962). The study by Block and Block (1951) that correlates anti-Semitism with a visual indicator of intolerance of ambiguity complements the basic Witkin formulation. The appeal of this line of investigation stems from the physiological and/or cognitive foundations upon which these theories of personality are based.

Research on the achievement motive (McClelland, Atkinson, Clark, and Lowell, 1953; McClelland, 1961) has had some very convincing independent validation, although Brody's (1972) critique of the causal inferences drawn by McClelland seems to be valid and casts some doubt upon the actual role of the achievement motive as a predictor of subsequent behavior.[13] The risk-taking model that has emerged from the achievement studies and from "expectancy" theories (Tolman, 1955; Feather, 1959) is intellectually more satisfying and more amenable to the (now successful) generation and testing of explicit hypotheses that devolve from the theory (Atkinson, 1957; Atkinson and Feather, 1966). The distinction between motives to achieve and motives to avoid failure, combined with the intervening variables of perceived probability of success and ascribed values to probable outcomes has realized a higher level of theoretical sophistication than was realized in the earlier achievement motive research. Atkinson and Feather (1966: 5) in the introduction to their edited review of achievement research clearly admit to the intellectual development of the risk-taking model:

> The [earlier] theory of achievement motivation is a minature system applied to a specific context, the domain of achievement-oriented activities, which is characterized by the fact that the individual is responsible for the outcome (success or failure), he anticipates unambiguous knowledge or results, and there is some degree of uncertainty or risk (McClelland, 1961). Yet it is our belief that the type of theory that views the strength of an individual's goal-directed tendency as jointly determined by his *motives,* by his *expectations* about the consequences of his actions, and by the *incentive values* of expected consequences will have wider utility when these concepts are applied to analysis of behavior in other kinds of situations directed toward other goals [Italics in original].

A final dichotomy that will be mentioned as possibly useful for political analysis is the open-closed mind dichotomy of Rokeach (1960). Not only does Rokeach's personality dimension overcome the "right-authoritarian bias" of earlier authoritarianism research, the earlier F-scale seems to mix psychological authoritarianism and political authoritarianism investigation without showing a prior correlation between these two types of authoritarianism (supra, p. 19).

While some (or all) of these personality trait constructs may eventually contribute to the explanation of elite behavior, their empirical verification and the theoretical interrelationships among them are beyond the scope of this study. Figure 2 offers a preliminary schematic of possible trait-state interactions, states here identified as "response modes." The present study is concerned with solely the response modes of political elites and their empirical identification and measurement. It may be the case that such response modes can endure and become "habits" or "predispositions to behavior." This seems to be Barber's central assumption. However, the present study concerns itself solely with response modes qua response modes.

These response modes will be more fully discussed later, but it is necessary to return again to our initial outline of the tasks of elite analysis in the context of international relations. As noted initially, one of the responsibilities of research is to present valid, reliable, empirical indices of the dimensions one wishes to investigate.

In the field of international relations, problems of measurement of elites can be broken down into major difficulties: (1) the problem of accessibility and (2) the problem of semantic equivalence. A subset of the semantic equivalence problem is the difficulty of interpreting elite responses, generally of a verbal form, that constitute masking of lying behavior.

Richard Brody (1969: 116) succinctly summarizes the problem of

[16]

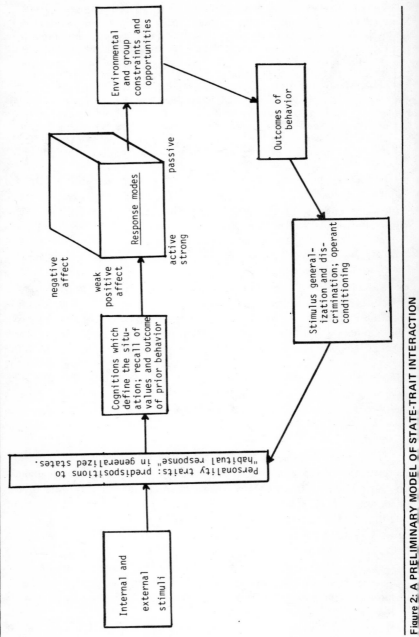

Figure 2: A PRELIMINARY MODEL OF STATE-TRAIT INTERACTION

accessibility when he asks: "[H]ow can we give a Taylor Manifest-Anxiety Scale to Khrushchev during the Hungarian revolt, a Semantic Differential to Chiang Kai-shek while Quemoy is being shelled, or simply interview Kennedy during the Cuban missle crisis?" Clearly, the answer to each part of this question is that we cannot. Students of international relations generally are excluded from gathering data on elites when those elites are engaged in the most crucial, salient, and theoretically important types of behavior.

The answer, of course, lies in utilizing the research methodology of content analysis. The consequent question is: what should we content analyze and what can we legitimately infer from the given analysis? The answer to this question is relatively clear, yet the full import of the answer seems not to have influenced recent attempts at elite analysis: *We should content analyze as many of those channels of communication which act as data sources, channels that include kinesic, audio, and linguistic forms of communication; we should draw inferences about general elite behavior only from comparative cross-national, cross-cultural data that fulfill the prerequisite of being semantically and/or behaviorally equivalent.*

Such semantic and/or behavioral equivalents constitute a vital and necessary arsenal for valid cross-national research efforts that look at either elite or mass behavior. Richard Merritt (1970: 152-153) has discussed the related problems of "syntactic" equivalence as well as semantic uniqueness. While these additional methodological problems are significant in conducting elite analysis in an international or cross-national framework, the fundamental problem of semantic equivalence is becoming increasingly salient to scholars in the field of comparative and international affairs. As Hymes (1970: 321) notes:

> The choice of a language, or of code level within a language, carries within it inevitably a semantic value, for the speech code will be associated in the minds of the respondents with the persons, purposes, and situations for which it is typically used. As the Spanish-Guaraní, Norwegian, and diglossia situations show, members of a community may themselves choose among speech codes to express these meanings, thus defining identities, intents, and occasions.

> Clearly it is not enough to know in a general way "the language of the country." To plan comparative research wisely, a scholar needs to know the set of languages and dialects; the semantic resources, topical scope, of each; the symbolic meaning of each. He needs to know, in short, how the standard verbal repertoire is organized and utilized.

The search for semantic equivalencies can be conducted in three ways: (1) through the use of highly sophisticated, often bilingual, translation codes (usually entailing "back-translation" as a check on the validity of the translation codes), (2) through the use of bipolar "naming" techniques (Osgood, 1957), and (3) through the investigation of "linguistic universals," i.e., characteristics of the encoding process, that then can be applied to specific national or cultural linguistic systems.

The first of these strategies works on the principle of matching specific words, phrases, or syntactic constructs from two or more language families under investigation. The second strategy attempts to have cross-national or cross-cultural respondents "locate" specific words within what Osgood calls the universal "semantic space." The third strategy involves comparing large numbers of language families in an attempt to find common underlying denominators and universal encoding patterns. These denominators and patterns are then brought to bear upon the specific linguistic system(s) under investigation.

The present study utilizes this third approach. A number of linguistic universals have been identified (Greenberg, 1962), generally at the syntactic level. Other linguistic or "paralinguistic" universals seem obviously to flow from physiological studies of language use and communication (Mahl, 1956; Goldman-Eisler, 1961, 1968). Psychological parameters that universally determine language utilization (Whorf, 1956; Brown and Lenneberg, 1954; Brown, 1965; Zipf, 1935, 1949) also have been either hypothesized and/or empirically verified. This is not the place to review general findings of this genre of studies. Such a review is available in a recent article by Miller and McNeill (1969). The theoretical relevance of these studies to the nonobtrusive analysis of political elites will be more fully investigated in Frank (1973a) and generally by Milburn and Herman (1974, forthcoming).

In terms of elite analysis, the point being made here is quite simple: cross-national or cross-cultural investigation requires that elite responses can be standardized and that the investigator has the linguistic tools by which he can establish the standardizing equivalencies. Not only in terms of accurately presenting the stimulus material in a survey or interview situations, but also in terms of accurately evaluating the subject's responses, such semantic equivalencies (or at the least such "transformation rules") constitute the sine qua non of in-depth elite analysis.

While there is evidence of the existence of syntactic universals, paralinguistic and kinesic universals, and physiological-psychological, language-use universals, the present study will look at specifically one type of previously undiscussed universal, i.e., universals of symbolic communication. As Merritt (1970: 71) notes: "Since man enshrouds so much of his behavior and thinking in symbolism, it only makes good sense to analyze his use of symbols." And it "makes good sense" for a series of reasons discussed above:

(1) Since man enshrouds his thinking in symbolism, the symbols that an individual uses should be "symptomatic" of more masked psychological states.

(2) Since men continuously interact within a symbolic nexus, since they justify behavior and appeal for support through the use of symbolic communication, the study of symbols can begin to tackle the problem of the level-of-analysis phenomenon in political explanation.

(3) Since there does seem to exist at least one major subset of symbolic communication that is universal, i.e., fulfills the requirement of semantic equivalence, at least this one subset of symbols should prove highly effective in cross-national elite analysis.

(4) Since a clear examination of state-analysis is (a) a more consensual level of psychometric assessment than deeper "trait" analysis and (b) easily tied through a learning-theoretic model to a more complex behavioral system, symptomatic symbols later should be found to be applicable (in terms of both receptivity to and utilization of) to socialization, recruitment, and a host of related psychopolitical phenomena.

The present study will analyze a specific subset of symbols that we call "spatially oriented" or simply "spatial" symbols. It is hypothesized that this cluster of symbols taps *positive or negative affect* that characterizes the situational psychological state of the given symbol user. (The positive-negative affect dimension is of course one of the three dimensions of "state response modes" diagrammed in Figure 2). It is furthermore assumed that the "symptomatic use" of spatially oriented symbols constitutes a symbolic universal, i.e., a symbolic response that is not culture bound and therefore fully consonant with the definitional requirements for cross-cultural semantic equivalence. It is furthermore assumed that such symbols are of great value when treated not only as indicators of personal (or psychological) states, but also when spatial symbols are treated as sociopolitical phenomena. Further examination of the use and receptivity towards spatial symbols not only can overcome the problem of levels-of-analysis in international studies, such symbols also should increase our understanding of specific political processes such as the mass acceptance of ideology, the recruitment of political leaders, the establishment of group cohesion, and other highly significant political behaviors.

While these subjects will be briefly covered at the conclusion of this paper, the main thrust of the present study is to establish the validity of utilizing spatial symbol analysis as an indicator, or symptom, of psychological affect on the part of the elite spatial symbol users. The data base for this examination will be primarily State of the Union messages given by presidents of the United States[14] during the twentieth century. Content validity will be established by correlating spatial symbols with frequencies of "non-immediate" object reference. (This notion of non-immediacy will be defined and operationalized later in this paper.) External validity for the notion of spatial symbols will be provided through correlations with paralinguistic data, specifically "verbal slip" data as defined by Mahl (1956). Furthermore, data manipulation utilizing grossly defined system stress (in a historical sense) will add further statistical evidence to the legitimacy and viability of spatial symbol analysis.

Before turning to data analysis, however, it will be necessary to review research and theory in disciplines somewhat removed from traditionally accepted domans of international relations research. The goal of this digression will be to present evidence for the existence of a phenomenon called "verbal kinesics" (Frank, 1972). Through a general theory of verbal kinesics one can extrapolate to the specific hypotheses as well as more fully understand the deductive process by which the notion of spatial symbols was evolved.

A THEORY OF VERBAL KINESICS

Over 170 years ago Destutt de Tracy (1801) coined the word "ideology" and claimed that the study of ideology was a part of the science of zoology since human thinking is a subset of animal life and therefore must be considered a subject of zoological concern (Stein, 1961). The theory of verbal kinesics explicated here builds upon this earliest assumption of the biological and behavioral foundations of language and therefore of symbolism. A number of recent studies have been devoted either entirely or in part to the biological foundations of language (Lenneberg, 1967; Chomsky, 1968: 58ff; Morton, 1970; Pribram, 1971; Piaget, 1971). Scholars of primate behavior also have popularized the notion of the prehuman origins of language (Andrew, 1963; Marshall, 1970). David Apter (1964: 20) in his discussion of the origins and function of ideology writes: "[I]deology, like language and dreams, is related to morphologies of behavior by universal psychobiological variables." For the individual, Apter argues that receptivity to ideology is at least in part tied to the process of maturation. Erikson (1958: 87) makes the same point in his discussion of Luther's acceptance of the philosophical teachings of Occam.

Apter (1964: 18-21) notes that an examination of metaphor and myth should be fruitful sources of information concerning the nature and the psychosocial functions of ideology (the functions of identity and solidarity). The analysis of metaphor and myth called for by Apter and by Geertz (1964: 57-58) has been attempted by Frank (1972). Furthermore, Apter, Geertz, and Frank have emphasized the importance of religious symbolism as perhaps the deepest form of ideological and symbolic thinking:

> One difference between religion and other forms of thought is that religion has more power. So fundamental is its power that one cannot examine individual conduct or desires without reference to it. In that sense religion cuts into human personality in a way in which ordinary ideological thought rarely does [Apter, 1968, originally 1963: 199].

If spatial symbols actually constitute a universal subset of symbolic communication, we should find such regularity in religious symbolism and in mythical expression. If spatial symbols are to be explained in terms of a theory of verbal kinesics (a theory that will be shown draws heavily upon the demonstrated universality of "nonlinguistic" kinesic behavior), then there should exist a body-symbolic as well as a "body-behavioral" core to accompany at least these forms of ideological and symbolic thought.

Religious as well as political symbolism is replete with body imagery. The function of this type of symbolism has been discussed by Brown (1959) from a psychoanalytical position, by Douglas (1970: 137-153) in terms of cognitive anthropology, and by Fisher and Cleveland (1968) from research in clinical psychology. A continuing theme through these works and in other literature too voluminous to cite here is that indeed one's body acts as an analogous model by which evaluations of the political and/or social system are made. Schwartz (1972) notes that high levels of prediction concerning an individual's preferred mode of political action can be obtained through an analysis of that individual's style of body maintenance behavior.

While the symptomatic as well as sociopolitical importance of the use and receptivity of these manifest forms of body imagery constitutes an important aspect of the theory of symbolic behavior, in terms of spatial symbols we are interested not so much in manifest forms of body imagery, but rather are concerned with *orienting and reacting dimensions contained in the metaphor of symbol and myth.* We shall argue that there are two such basic dimensions, a "horizontal dimension" (e.g., flight symbols, general escape or horizontal movement [such as the imagery of the pilgrim] symbols) and "a vertical dimension" (e.g., themes of ascension, symbols of height).[15] Furthermore, if one agrees with Langer (1942: 54-75) that the essence of metaphor is meaning standing for more than itself, then the deeper meaning or the "deep metaphor" of these spatial symbols is intimately connected with the notion of body imagery and specifically with the body-behavioral predispositions of the symbol user.[16]

In other words, an increase of negative affect (or stress) for an individual predisposes that individual to actual physical flight. He wants to respond behaviorally to a negatively valued situation or object by moving or "distantiating" his body away from the stress-producing stimulus. In many cases this behavioral response is impossible. There is "no way out," social sanctions or situational sanctions preclude this possibility; for various reasons such a behavioral response is impossible. Linguistic response does not operate within such sanctions. Under conditions of stress, the individual can respond linguistically by choosing to use symbolism that reflects the directionality of the unavailable behavioral response, in this case by using "horizontal symbols." [17]

We shall return to this line of reasoning later in this paper. Even if this linguistic-semantic phenomenon is valid, in terms of generating a cross-cultural psychological state indicator it must be shown that such linguistic-semantic "spatiality" is indeed universal and semantically equivalent.

The evidence from comparative religious and cultural anthropological research overwhelmingly confirms the existence and semantic equivalence of these spatial dimensions in one culture and religion after another. Eliade (1960: 99-122) carefully documents the universality and universal meaning of the "ascension theme," notes the cosmological significance of the symbol of the king with upraised arms (1963: 39-40), and ties the notion of "construction rites" with the symbolism of cosmological origin (1959: 15-16).[18] Hans Jonas' (1963) study of the gnostic movement in pre- and early-Christian times emphasizes the symbolic importance of both the "fall" (and eventual ascension) and the messenger. Daniel Ogilvie (1969) through the use of factor analytic techniques has shown the cross-cultural importance of differences in the "individual and cultural patterns of fantasized flight." Haller (1957) and Walzer (1968) have shown the symbolic power and widespread utilization of flight symbols during the Puritan Revolution in Europe, a revolution that marked not only the ideological overthrow of the feudal social and political systems but also the complete reorientation of fundamental religious and social thought.

A number of anthropologists and psychologists have shown the necessity for an integrated balance of vertical and horizontal movements in the behavioral patterns of mythic heroes (Rank, 1959; Campbell, 1949, 1968; Levi-Strauss, 1966, 1967, especially 1967a, 1969 [see Leach, 1969]; Turner, 1969; Kluckhohn, 1968). In short, the universality of these spatial dimensions as key ingredients to mythic structures has been very well documented.

We do have evidence of a symbolic universal, i.e., spatial symbols, that can be applied directly to the analysis of political rhetoric and that can guarantee maintenance of semantic equivalence. In the above discussion, we introduced the notion of linguistic displacements of behavioral predispositions. In order to offer a psychological explanation of this cross-cultural symbol patterning, we shall briefly review two key studies: (1) Leach's (1964) etymological study of the origins of obscene words in the English language, and (2) Wiener and Mehrabian's (1968) experiments with levels of non-immediacy in referential pronouns, use of passive voice, and sentence phrase modifiers.[19] We will then be in a position to present a theory of verbal kinesics, tie this theory to the phenomenon of spatial symbols, and then turn directly to our data analysis.

Leach (1964: 23) begins his discussion of verbal abuse by clearly stating that he is working with the hypothesis of repression of semantic boundary percepts.

> When psychologists debate about the mechanism of "forgetting" they often introduce the concept of "interference," the idea that there is a tendency to repress concepts that have some kind of semantic overlap (Postman, 1961). The thesis which I present depends upon a converse hypothesis, namely, that we can only arrive at semantically distinct verbal concepts if we repress the boundary percepts that lie between them.

Some of the boundary percepts that Leach works with are those such as dietary restrictions, the seminal treatment of which remains Douglas' (1970: 54-72) cognitive-behavioral analysis of the dietary restrictions in the Books of Leviticus and Deuteronomy. While the origins of these dietary restrictions have much in common with the behavioral-linguistic phenomenon under investigation here, Leach's origin of dirty words is a much more striking example and one which will suffice here.

Leach (1964) discusses the relationship between behavioral and linguistic taboos and notes that (unlike his dietary restrictions) certain taboos, mainly sexual, can originate either in the behavioral or in the linguistic domains of human experience.

> Linguistic taboos and behavioral taboos are not only sanctioned in the same way, they are very much muddled up: sex behavior and sex words, for example. But this association of deed and word is not so simple as might appear. The relationship is not necessarily causal. It is not the case that certain kinds of behavior are taboo and that, therefore, the language relating to such behavior becomes taboo. Sometimes words may be taboo in themselves for linguistic (phonemic) reasons, and the causal link, if any, is then reversed; a behavioral taboo comes to reflect a prior verbal taboo [pp. 24-25].

In short, *words have an existence, a function, stimulus properties of their own. Not only do words act as cognitive reflections, conscious communications, of wholly independent acts, they can themselves determine the nature and direction of future acts. Of crucial importance is the fact that the relationship between words and deeds is a mutually interactive one, and in some cases there is a one-to-one correspondence between physical behavior and linguistic behavior.* We all know that words themselves can hurt, comfort, embarrass, please, amuse, and effect a large number of behavioral responses. In the case of verbal obscenity, Leach demonstrates the cultural manipulation, avoidance, and pairing of words with deeds.

A few examples will clarify this point. Leach notes the English homonyms "queen" and "quean," the former is a word identifying positive virtue (the queen of England, queen bees), while the latter is a word that formerly meant prostitute and that now denotes a homosexual male and/or a barren cow. The obscenity "son of a bitch" has direct etymological connections with "dog" (God spelled backwards, with the connotations of "dog" being directly traceable to the highmark of the period of witches in English history) and with "goddamn" (God's animal mother). Thus we can see why "you son of a bitch" can have very pronounced connotative effects, whereas "you polar bear" or "you son of a cat" do not.[20]

There is a similar phonetic resemblance between "venery" (the archaic legal expression for beasts of game) and "venerate." Of importance is the fact that the term "venery" had alternative meanings, i.e., hunting and sexual indulgence. Thus, venery and venerate have connotations of sex and authority, both of which are sources of taboo (and respect) but in contrary senses.

For hundreds of years in the English culture the most powerful ritual of hunting has been fox hunting. Only a slight vowel shift in "fox" is necessary to produce "fux." As Leach (1964: 27) notes: "No doubt there is a sense in which such facts as these can be deemed linguistic accidents, but they are accidents which have a functional utility in the way we use our language." Men can hunt foxes, they can "be on the prowl" and/or procure sexual indulgence from women. In the ritual nomenclature of the fox hunt, the fox itself is a "dog" (while the dogs are called "hounds"), and the face of the fox is a "mask" (male sexual insecurity?) and the tail of the fox is called a "brush" (eliminating the "r" results in a contemporary slang description of the female genital area).

Similar cultural sanctions and/or identifications occur with the word horse (or eating horsemeat). In English, "horse" is often shortened to "orse" and even to "oss." Again, only a slight vowel change is necessary to produce "ass." Thus, not only can men "get into the saddle" and "ride" women, eating "horsemeat" is taboo in the English-American culture (although not necessarily so in other culture-linguistic systems). Likewise, the "bunny" as a Playboy symbol and as a general sexual symbol in American culture has linguistic antecedents. What we call a "rabbit" today in eighteenth-century England was called a "coney" (the etymological derivation being the Latin *cuniculus*), as Leach notes, a word that is "awkwardly close to *cunt* which only became printable in English with the licensed publication of *Lady Chatterley's Lover.*" (Leach, 1964: 50).

The purpose of this discussion of linguistic taboo is certainly not to shock or to titillate the reader (obviously, any serious student of language neither would be shocked nor titillated), instead, a very important point is being made about the characteristics of language. *Language, whether symbolically or through phonetic combinations, often plays a macro-political and a social function of determining cultural taboos. Furthermore, at the micro-political and psychological level, manipulation and perceptual boundary re-ordering (semantically) defines values, creates cognitive and behavioral isomorphs, and most importantly expresses symptomatic orientations of the language user toward his cultural, political, and biological environment.*

The above discussion of verbal obscenity and linguistic behavioral taboo leads us to at least one major conclusion, i.e., that the behavioral and psychological dimensions of language use must be reevaluated and that these dimensions must be granted a more autonomous and powerful place in social as well as psychological behavioral explanations. A major thrust in this direction is presented by Wiener and Mehrabian (1968) with their experimental explorations into the phenomenon they call "immediacy."

In short, Wiener and Mehrabian consider language as a "second order experience," i.e., an actual psychobehavioral process. While Leach considers language as a tool in the construction of social and personal reality, Wiener and Mehrabian treat certain forms of linguistic discourse *as an available psychological tool by which the language user can cope with negatively valued objects or situations by psycholinguistically distantiating the self and the negatively valued object or situation.*

Much like Leach, Wiener and Mehrabian assume an intimate *mutually interactive* relationship between thought, language, and behavior.[21] For Wiener and Mehrabian, a desired physical and/or psychological distantiation has its symptoms in the language that the individual uses.[22] For example, as I sit here typing this manuscript there is a cup of coffee on my desk approximately two feet away from my body. If someone came into the room and asked me what kind of coffee was in the cup, there are at least two types of linguistically acceptable responses: (1) "*This* is Brazilian ground coffee from a delicatessen in Philadelphia." (2) "*That* is Brazilian ground coffee from a delicatessen in Philadelphia." Both sentences are identical with the exception of one word, i.e., "this" or "that." The latter utilization is an example of what Wiener and Mehrabian would call "non-immediate language," and they have shown that the use of such non-immediate references is strongly correlated with subject negative-evaluation of the object of reference.

Other forms of non-immediate discourse work on the same principle, i.e., the tendency to "distantiate" linguistically negatively valued objects of reference. Without any change or difference in the actual physical locations of self and object of reference, linguistic (semantic) distantiation can create the psychologically desired distance. Such distantiation can take other forms such as inclusion of the self in a larger group (thus moving the object of reference away from the self). For example, if my friends and I go to Shea stadium to see the Mets play the Pittsburgh Pirates and the Mets are winning 10-0 (and I'm a Pirates fan), if someone asks me if I'm having a good time I might respond, "Yes, we're all having a good time." On the other hand, if the Pirates are winning 10-0, I might respond, "Yes, I'm having a good time." There of course will be other differences in my responses in each of these two situations. My answer may be more emphatic; I may accompany my response with additional kinesic emphasis or behavior, or whatever, but in terms of non-immediacy, the choice of "we're" instead of "I am" would be an instance of non-immediacy.

Examples of vertical and horizontal spatial symbols, non-immediate references, and body imagery are presented in Appendix 1. For complete definitions of the coding rules used in this study, consult Frank (1972).

The preceding discussion has attempted to make perfectly clear one specific assumption of this study, i.e., that indeed verbal behavior can have an inner logic, an "inner life"[23] and a specific set of psychological functions in which language acts as both tool and symptom that accompany states of psychological affect. At this point, we can formally state a theory of verbal kinesics and list the hypotheses that flow from this theory. We call the theory "verbal" because it deals with language use, and we call the theory "kinesics" because the language use in question is isomorphic with behavioral predispositions. Furthermore, the kinesic universals (of a non-verbal sense) that have been identified by Ekman, Friesen, and others seem to point to certain universal common denominators that underlie all types of kinesic activity. (See Ekman and Friesen, 1969, 1971; Ekman, Friesen and Ellsworth, 1972; Wiener, Devoe, Rubinow, and Geller, 1972; Eibl-Eibesfeldt, 1970; Ekman, 1972; Darwin, 1965.)

The theory of verbal kinesics as presented in this paper is as follows:

> *Certain semantic forms, including spatial symbols and referential distantiation, universally appear in verbal discourse. These semantic forms represent psycholinguistic tools by which body-environment and body-behavioral responses can be actualized. As such, these forms are symptomatic of underlying psychological states and are isomorphic with parallel behavioral dispositions. For example, under periods of stress the frequency of flight or horizontal symbols used by the speaker will increase as the predisposition to actual physical flight increases. This phenomenon can be accounted for by the overlapping of perceptual boundaries of language, thought, and behavior. Without postulating whether or not the needs that generated the responses are necessarily satisfied, the theory of verbal kinesics assumes that language behavior can replace physical responses which are effected by prior positively or negatively valued stimuli.*

As such, the theory of verbal kinesics in part attempts to operationalize the individual's "boundary definition" and "boundary maintenance" behaviors. The theory of verbal kinesics attempts to show how the language user establishes through the use of symbols a body-environment fit as described by Lifton (1967: 54-55): "For if we view man as primarily a symbol-forming organism, we must realize that he has a constant need for a meaningful inner formulation of self and world, in which his actions, and even his impulses, have some kind of 'fit' with the 'outside' as he perceives it."

The theory of verbal kinesics argues that under conditions of stress, the individual can employ two psycholinguistically distantiating strategies: (1) move the stressor away from the self through the use of non-immediate language, and (2) move the self away from the stressor through the use of horizontal movement symbols. Thus, the first hypothesis to be tested is:

(1) Under conditions of stress, there should exist statistically significant increases in the use of horizontal symbols and non-immediate references, and both of these linguistic forms should be highly correlated.

Since spatial symbols and non-immediate references ultimately can be explained in terms of body-environment relationships, a second hypothesis presents itself:

(2) Under conditions of stress, in addition to increases in the use of spatial symbols and non-immediate references, there should be a parallel increase in the use of body imagery that reflects the concern for the self in the face of threat or anxiety.

Furthermore, since spatial symbols and non-immediate references are generated by negatively valued objects or situations, it should be the case that the use of such linguistic forms is "topic free." In other words:

(3) The use of spatial symbols and non-immediate references should not be correlated with any specific object of communication (i.e., any specific political topic or issue), but rather should be correlated only with those situational topics or issues that at the moment are negatively valued and therefore that are stress-producing.

Finally, in order to establish construct validity, a fourth hypothesis should be tested:

(4) The use of spatial symbols should be correlated with non-semantic measures of stress such as verbal slips and speech rate indicators.

We now turn to a description of this research and to the results of our analysis.

ANALYSIS OF DATA

In order to test the four hypotheses, a content analysis was done on State of the Union messages of presidents of the United States. State of the Union messages were chosen (1) on the assumption that this would control for audience, format of presentation, and other situational variables and (2) because it was assumed that these messages would be highly symbolic while at the same time totally authored (or highly supervised) by the presidents themselves. For State of the Union messages, there is ample testimony by former speech writers and journalists, as well as extensively "worked over" drafts, to support this assumption (see Frank, 1972). Moreover, since State of the Union messages rarely, if ever, announce broad new policies, the extensive research and writing from many sources (such as characterized the writing of the Truman doctrine [see Jones, 1955: 148-170]) is not in operation here. In short, the State of the Union messages are assumed to be symbolic and personal. A categorization of "speech types" is presented in Figure 3.

Speeches of presidents of the United States were chosen for a series of reasons: (1) the historical as well as political importance of presidents of the United States during the twentieth century, (2) the elimination of any possible translation errors and difficulties, (3) the prior development of the non-immediacy protocol by Wiener and Mehrabian using English-language-speaking subjects, and (4) the desire to minimize role differences and to control for role occupancy across many decades of American political life. All coding was done manually by students of Allentown College and the University of Pennsylvania. Coding categories and instructions for coding were established manually. While the alternative approach would have been the establishment of content categories using factor analytic techniques, serious theoretical problems still remain in moving from this latter technique to the establishment of valid content categories (Stone, 1969: 523-537). The Israel text (1967) was used in the textual content analysis and audio tapes of available State of the Union

	Significant Speech	Nonsignificant Speech
Policy Change Speech	Ghosted Authorship e.g., Truman doctrine; Quarantine speech (FDR)	(undefined set)
Traditional Reaffirmation Speech	Presidential Authorship e.g., State of the Union; Inaugural; nomination acceptance	Ghosted Authorship e.g., welcome to Washington and to the White House; speeches to civic groups; brief political anniversary day speeches, or press releases

Figure 3: A TYPOLOGICAL DESCRIPTION OF TYPES OF PRESIDENTIAL COMMUNICATION

TABLE 1
VERTICAL, HORIZONTAL, BODY IMAGE AND NONIMMEDIACY SCORES FOR 38 STATE OF THE UNION MESSAGES, 1934-1969

Message by President	V.	H.	V/H	Date	NI	BI	Pp.	NI Pp.	BI Pp.
FDR									
1	8	15	.53	1/34	12	0	4.00	3.00	.00
2	9	13	.69	1/35	16	4	6.00	2.67	.67
3	4	9	.44	1/36	30	5	6.50	4.62	.76
4	3	9	.33	1/37	23	2	4.75	4.84	.42
5	1	4	.25	1/38	34	6	8.50	4.00	.70
6	4	10	.40	1/39	25	5	7.00	3.57	.71
7	4	9	.44	1/40	15	9	5.75	2.61	1.56
8	3	7	.43	1/41	17	8	6.00	2.83	1.33
9	3	8	.38	1/42	20	4	6.00	3.33	.67
10	4	7	.56	1/43	14	5	8.00	1.75	.62
11	4	5	.80	1/44	14	2	6.75	2.07	.30
12	11	6	1.83	1/45	16	7	15.00	1.07	.47
HST									
1	15	16	.94	1/46	48	27	31.00	1.55	.87
2	4	3	1.33	1/47	12	3	11.50	1.04	.26
3	14	19	.74	1/48	14	6	9.50	1.47	.63
4	6	14	.43	1/49	11	6	6.25	1.76	.96
5	10	18	.55	1/50	20	6	8.75	2.29	.70
6	12	19	.63	1/51	19	9	7.50	2.53	1.20
7	11	27	.41	1/52	25	10	9.50	2.63	1.05
8	18	32	.56	1/53	24	18	17.00	1.41	1.06
DDE									
1	3	10	.30	2/53	35	9	13.75	2.55	.65
2	10	11	.91	1/54	18	6	12.25	1.47	.49
3	11	11	1.00	1/55	13	5	13.50	.96	.37
4	10	16	.62	1/56	18	4	15.50	1.16	.26
5	7	10	.70	1/57	8	7	7.75	1.03	.90
6	10	14	.71	1/58	11	1	10.00	1.10	.10
7	10	10	1.00	1/59	11	3	9.75	1.13	.32
8	11	15	.73	1/60	10	6	10.75	.93	.56
9	9	6	1.50	1/61	8	1	13.00	.62	.08
JFK									
1	3	9	.33	1/61	20	2	9.75	2.05	.20
2	17	15	1.13	1/62	22	2	11.50	1.91	.17
3	8	22	.36	1/68	19	3	10.00	1.90	.30
LBJ									
1	3	4	.75	1/64	13	2	5.75	2.26	.35
2	8	26	.31	1/65	19	6	9.50	2.00	.63
3	6	24	.25	1/66	36	10	10.75	3.26	.93
4	18	27	.67	1/67	37	12	18.00	2.06	.67
5	5	7	.71	1/68	29	3	13.00	2.23	.23
6	1	12	.08	1/69	32	4	11.25	2.84	.35

broadcasts were donated by the Columbia Broadcasting System. Both intercoder and intracoder reliabilities consistently exceeded .80 using the Holsti (1969: 140) reliability formula. Since there were no force-choice coding strategies employed in this study, additional correction factors for random placement were not considered.

For the major series of coded speeches, i.e., 38 State of the Union messages from Franklin D. Roosevelt through Lyndon Johnson (inclusive), spatial symbols, non-immediacy, and body imagery frequency counts are taken. For the non-immediacy scores (hereafter referred to as NI scores) and for the body image frequencies (hereafter referred to as BI scores), speech length is controlled. "Wide spacing" on certain pages of the Israel text is also controlled. Speeches given after the publication of the Israel text were taken from *Vital Speeches* and converted into Israel page equivalents.

In working with the spatial symbols, no such correction for speech length was necessary. A very simple ratio is used to ascertain the frequencies of vertical and horizontal symbol use. Our "V/H ratio" gives the number of vertical symbols used for a given unit of text divided by the number of horizontal symbols used for that same unit of text. Thus, *the higher the real number of the V/H ratio, the greater the use of vertical to horizontal symbols, and therefore the lower the hypothesized stress level of the symbol user. Conversely, the smaller the value of the real number, the greater the use of horizontal symbols to vertical symbols, and therefore the higher the hypothesized stress level of the symbol user.*

The results of the speech coding are presented in Table 1.

Because we are dealing with results generated by content analysis, results subject to some measurement error due to coding disagreements, we decided to treat this data as ordinal level rather than admittedly more statistically powerful interval data. Therefore, rank-order correlations and chi-square distributions are used as our primary statistical tools.

The correlation between V/H ratios and NI Scores was .731 (p < .01). The predicted correlation was obtained. (Unless otherwise stated, all cited correlations are Spearman rank-order correlations.)

Thus in the first sample of 38 State of the Union messages, there seems to exist internal consistency and fluctuations of our indicator variables. In order to establish external validity, two procedures were adopted. First, the 38 speeches were divided into two historical groups: (1) "depression-war" speeches and (2) "prosperity-peace" speeches. The depression-war speeches included those State of the Union messages from 1934-1944, 1951-1953, and 1965-1969, inclusive (n=20). We took the liberty of disallowing the Roosevelt State of the Union message of 1945 for two reasons: (1) by January 1945 it was fairly certain that the Allies were going to win the war within a matter of months[24] and (2) as Burns (1970: 36, 352-353) notes, the unprecedented fourth-term mandate given to Roosevelt only two months before had had a great "uplifting" effect on the president.

The other 18 speeches, the "propserity-peace" speeches, were likewise grouped together. It is hypothesized that the V/H ratios would be lower for the depression-war speeches than for the prosperity-peace speeches. Only one assumption is made here, i.e., that war and depression are stressful situations. [25]

These speeches were rank-ordered according to V/H ratios and then categorized as either prosperity-peace or depression-war speeches. A Mann-Whitney U test was conducted on this data. With n_1 and n_2 of 19, the resultant U of 57 is significant at the .002 level (two-tailed test). Horizontal to vertical symbol use increases, as predicted, in speeches given during periods of depression and/or war.

We also wished to investigate the use of body imagery during these speeches, for the theory of verbal kinesics argues that under conditions of stress there also will be an increase in the use of body image rhetoric. It should be noted in passing that use of body image rhetoric is a slightly more complex theoretical framework. While both non-immediacy and spatial symbol use are examples of one type or another of distantiating strategy, concern for the self is a nondistantiating phenomenon. While body image rhetoric fits the paradigm of verbal kinesics, its full explication is beyond the scope of this paper. The reader is referred to Frank (1973b).

We conducted a Mann-Whitney U test on the body image scores in which a rank-ordering of body image score/pages was categorized along the peace-prosperity and war-depression categories as described above. As predicted, the speeches with high body image references were associated in statistically significant fashion with speeches given during conditions of national economic depression and/or involvement in international war. The probability under H_o of achieving the distribution of crisis and noncrisis speeches along the rank-ordering of body image scores was .02 (two-tailed test).

Moreover, we tested the strength of association between body image scores and horizontal and vertical symbol use. Returning to the data in Table 1, if all vertical and horizontal symbol frequencies are summed, the resulting total V/H proportion for all speeches is .589. The mean BI Score per page of Israel text for these same speeches is .588. Using these two figures as cut-off points, a 2 X 2 matrix was established and a median test

TABLE 2

MEDIAN TEST ON V/H AND BI DATA USING STATE OF THE UNION SAMPLE

	BI Above .588	BI Below .588
V/H Below .597	15	4
V/H Above .597	6	13

was conducted on the BI data (Siegel, 1956: 111-115). The resulting BI distribution is presented in Table 2.

The resulting chi-square value was 6.812, df = 1 (p $<$ .01). From these results we conclude that, as predicted from the theory of verbal kinesics, the use of body image symbolism is significantly associated with an increase in the ratio of horizontal to vertical symbol use.

One might wish to argue that such spatial symbols do not form the basis of an independent theory of verbal kinesics but rather they simply act as intervening variables or indicators, predicated not upon levels of actor stress, but rather simply "naturally" associated with specific topics such as domestic or foreign affairs. According to such a competing formulation, for example, one might argue that horizontal symbols are naturally associated with foreign relations and vertical symbols associated with domestic affairs. A Mann-Whitney U test of the domestic and foreign V/H scores associated with the speeches in this set obtained a z-score of .239 where the formula for the computation of the Mann-Whitney U with n_2 greater than 20 was taken from Siegel (1956). There is no statistically significant association of types of spatial symbols with either domestic or foreign topics.

However, when we grouped all issue areas into crisis or noncrisis categories (war-depression versus peace-prosperity) and took only the V/H scores for that aspect of each speech that dealt with this crisis area, we did obtain significant results. We went back to our original data from the State of the Union messages, 1934-1969, and found *separate* V/H ratios for those aspects of the addresses concerning foreign affairs. From this set of State of the Union messages, we then ascertained which addresses were given during periods of national war and/or depression and ascertained from this "depression-war" subset whether the national crisis was of a domestic or of a foreign nature. These results are presented in Table 3.

We then found the mean V/H score for all speech contexts, domestic or foreign, that were deemed stressful and compared the results with mean V/H scores of the remainder of the "noncrisis" category entries, i.e., the "alternative" category (domestic or foreign) to that category that was

TABLE 3
COMPARATIVE V/H RATIOS FOR DOMESTIC AND FOREIGN
CONTEXTS, STATE OF THE UNION MESSAGES, 1934-1969

Year	Message by President	Domestic V/H	Foreign V/H
1934	FDR 1	.31*	2.00
1935	2	.64*	1.00
1936	3	.33*	.67
1937	4	.29*	.50
1938	5	.25*	1.00
1939	6	.11*	3.00
1940	7	4.00	.11*
1941	8	.25	.67*
1942	9	.50	.33*
1943	10	1.00	.40*
1944	11	1.00	.50*
1945	12	5.00	1.17
1946	HST 1	.75	1.12
1947	2	2.00	1.00
1948	3	.92	.43
1949	4	56	.20
1950	5	.31	1.20
1951	6	.50	.69*
1952	7	.25	.47*
1953	8	.57	.88*
1953	DDE 1	.28	.33*
1954	2	1.14	.50
1955	3	1.12	.67
1956	4	.78	.43
1957	5	1.25	.33
1958	6	2.00	.50
1959	7	.83	1.25
1960	8	.67	.83
1961	9	1.00	2.50
1961	JFK 1	.67	.17
1962	2	1.33	1.00
1963	3	.67	.25
1964	LBJ 1	.67	1.00
1965	2	.58	.07*
1966	3	.25	.25*
1967	4	.58	.73*
1968	5	1.00	.75*
1969	6	.33	.10*

* Represents that context determined to be that of crisis.

TABLE 4
ANALYSIS OF CRISIS SPEECHES, STATE OF THE UNION
MESSAGES, 1934-1969, DIFFERENTIATED INTO "CRISIS" AND
"ALTERNATIVE" V/H SCORES AND THEIR RESPECTIVE MEANS

Date	V/H of Stressful Context	V/H of "Alternative" Score
1934	.31	2.00
1935	.64	1.00
1936	.33	.67
1937	.29	.50
1928	.25	1.00
1939	.11	3.00
1940	.11	4.00
1941	.67	.25
1942	.33	.50
1943	.40	1.00
1944	.50	1.00
1951	.69	.50
1952	.47	.25
1953	.88	.57
1953	.33	.28
1965	.07	.58
1966	.25	.25
1967	.73	.58
1968	.75	1.00
1969	.10	.33
(n=20)	$\overline{X} = .41$	$\overline{X} = .96$

deemed a topic of political crisis. These crisis topics are marked with an asterisk in Table 3. In Table 4 we collected all crisis categories by speech and all "alternative" categories by speech, found the grand means for the crisis and the alternative categories, and conducted difference of means tests for related measures. The results are presented in Table 4.

As the results clearly demonstrate, spatial symbol patterns do shift, with statistical significance, internal to speeches according to the degree of perceived topic-stress on the part of the speech giver. The use of either vertical or horizontal symbols is not "topic bound," as the theory of verbal kinesics would predict they would not be.

While the concept of referential non-immediacy has had extensive external validation, a final phase of this part of our study attempted to contribute even further external evidence to the validity of using spatial symbols as symptomatic indicators of levels of stress and direction of affect. For a subset of the 38 speeches analyzed in Table 1, there exist audio recordings of the speeches themselves. Therefore, we compared linguistic-semantic behavior with forms of paralinguistic behavior, specifically with speech rate and rate of "verbal slips" for the available speeches.

TABLE 5
RANK ORDER OF TOPIC STRESS ESTABLISHED USING PARALINGUISTIC INDICATOR

EISENHOWER

Message 1: (1953)
1. Military Efficiency .445
2. Conclusion .425
3. Foreign Policy .249
4. Loyalty Program .226

Message 3: (1955)
1. International Trade and Aid .498
2. Agriculture .313
3. Economy .219

Message 5: (1957)
1. Conclusion .282
2. International Affairs .237

Message 6: (1958)[a]
1. Communist Menace .241
2. Military Strength .238
3. Defense Reorganization .221
4. Science, Education, Research .230

Message 7: (1959)[a]
1. Economy .222
2. Military Strength .220

Message 8: (1960)[a]
1. Labor, Agriculture, Inflation .259
2. HEW .247
3. Government Spending .220
4. Military Strength .211

KENNEDY

Message 2: (1962)
1. Inflation .287
2. Foreign Policy .266
3. UN Peacekeeping .223
4. International Economics .216

Message 3: (1963)
1. HEW .203

JOHNSON

Message 2: (1965)
1. Conclusion .424
2. Non-Communist World .306
3. Toward Great Society .250

Message 3: (1966)
1. HEW, Government Efficiency .276
2. Vietnam .274

Message 4: (1967)
1. Vietnam .203

Message 5: (1968)
1. Conclusion .361
2. Foreign Policy .356
3. Introduction .289
4. Vietnam .275
5. Economy .255

Message 6: (1969)
1. Vietnam, Mid-East .531
2. HEW .494
3. Budget and Inflation .493
4. Introduction .277
5. Foreign Affairs .260

NIXON

Message 1: (1970)
1. Inflation .222
2. Vietnam .216

Message 2: (1971)
1. HEW .493
2. Economics .217

a. Corrected for stroke.

While in one sense we are dealing here with two possibly different (although assumed related) types of psychological stress, i.e., situational and dispositional stress (Lazarus, 1966: 197-209),[26] stress responses as manifested in V/H ratios should parallel stress responses manifested in paralinguistic behavior. Our measure of paralinguistically manifested stress is a multiplicative[27] combination of Mahl's (1956) verbal slip protocol and Murray's (U-curve hypotheses, 1971) findings on changing speech rate as a function of personal stress. We measured paralinguistically manifested stress utilizing the following formula: $\text{Stress}_{\text{pl}}$ = (time in seconds) (speech disturbances)/(word length of document)^2.[28] Audio tapes were obtained for Eisenhower, Kennedy, Johnson, and Nixon State of the Union broadcasts, and V/H ratios for these speeches were generated and compared with the paralinguistic indicators. We controlled for the aphasia resulting from Eisenhower's 1957 stroke.[29]

We then rank-ordered, by speech, those topics internal to the speeches that generated a paralinguistic stress score greater than .200 (an arbitrary cut-off point). The changes in rank-orders from speech to speech and from president to president give added evidence (in terms of historical assessment) to the great deal of experimental validation that lies behind the verbal slip and the speech rate measures. The changing rank-orders are quite predictable given the historical realities of the ending of the Cold War, Sputnik, and the development of the Vietnam involvement.[30] These paralinguistic rank-orders are presented in Table 5.

Comparing the audio and the textual channels of communication, we worked with the hypothesis that V/H ratios, indicators of dispositional stress, should be a necessary precondition (if not a sufficient causal explanation) for the presence of high levels of paralinguistically manifested situational stress. Using Tukey's stem-and-leaf method (1970: especially Chapters 2, 4, and 5), we ascertained which of the speech topics showed "significant" levels of paralinguistic stress. We then ascertained the frequency distribution of "outside points" (statistically significant "tailers") for our V/H scores for the similar speeches.

In other words, we wanted to look at the distributions of significant stress scores using both linguistic-semantic and paralinguistic indicators. Our reasoning was rather straightforward: *What is the probability of obtaining the bimodal distribution of high stress scores on both indicators which indeed resulted?* If there was no association between linguistic and paralinguistic stress, "high" and "low" scores on one measure should be unassociated with "high" and "low" scores on the other measure.[31]

By taking the probability of outside points on both indicators clustering bimodally as they did, we conducted a binomial test on the resultant data. It was ascertained that the probability of such a distribution of paralinguistic outside points, above and below the V/H mean (which we used as the cut-off point as in the median test), a distribution of "1" and "7" respectively, under H_0 to be $p < .05$.[32] There does exist a clear and firm relationship between preconditional "dispositional" stress (as measured by V/H scores) and a more immediate "situational" stress (as measured by our paralinguistic indicator). These results do add external validity to the theory of verbal kinesics by presenting confirmatory evidence of the fact that V/H ratios are associated with levels of stress, the confirmatory evidence being obtained through analysis not internally contained within the procedure of textual content analysis.

Before turning to an historical-political analysis using the V/H ratios that we have attempted to validate and to explain here, one last minor study should be reported. Although in previous sections of this paper evidence was presented that argued that across a span of centuries, even millenia, spatial symbols do seem to indicate certain psychological or psychocultural states, it could be argued that since to this point we have been dealing with twentieth-century data, the resulting "styles" of communicating are simply a time and culture bound anomaly.

Therefore, it was decided to code the State of the Union messages of Abraham Lincoln for all three indices, NI, BI, and V/H. In the case of Lincoln, we confess to choosing the most critical period of the nineteenth century. Thus, at least as heuristic results prior to further investigation, the hypothesized extremity of this sample hopefully will counteract to some degree its brevity.

It was hypothesized that with the Lincoln sample, the V/H scores would fall below the "depression-war" mean V/H score cited previously. It was further hypothesized that the V/H proportion would decline from 1861 to 1862 as Lincoln realized that the "insurrection" was not going to be easily crushed. The State of the Union message of 1864 was hypothesized to have the highest V/H proportion of the speech set of 1862, 1863, and 1864 (realization that the war is going to be won by the North), while we hypothesized that all scores in the three-speech set would have lower V/H ratios than the 1861 speech.

Coding was done on V/H, NI, and BI indices. The results are presented in Table 6.

For the most part, the data fell in expected patterns with the exception of the third speech. It is interesting to note, however, that (if a president's own words can be believed) Lincoln in the body of this 1863 speech stated that "the crisis which threatened to divide the friends of the Union is now

TABLE 6
V/H, NI, AND BI SCORING, LINCOLN'S STATE OF THE
UNION MESSAGE

Message by President	V.	H.	V/H	Date	NI	BI	NI+BI Pp.	BI Pp.	Pp.
Lincoln									
1	5	5	1.00	12/61	22	5	1.96	.36	16.50
2	2	7	.28	12/62	36	12	2.91	.73	13.75
3	14	6	2.33	12/63	23	5	2.29	.48	12.25
4	9	10	.90	12/64	20	7	2.08	.54	13.00

past" (Israel, 1967: II, 1094). If indeed Lincoln did miscalculate the termination date of the Civil War, this could account for the higher V/H score.

We can observe two V/H scores below 1.00 indicating that the V/H phenomenon is more than a stylistic preference of twentieth-century politicians. The 1862 V/H score is among the lowest we recorded, although the number of spatial symbols is somewhat low for this speech. We also have some indication as to why the first V/H score did not dip below 1.00. In Lincoln's words as he spoke in retrospect of those first months of civil war, he noted that "for a long time it had been hoped that the rebellion could be suppressed without resorting to it as a military measure" (Israel, 1967: II, 1094). Obviously, by December 1862, this hope had long since faded, and the V/H ratio of this second State of the Union message dropped accordingly. The distribution of the body image references was very satisfying. Using the matrix parameters presented in Table 2, the BI score of every Lincoln speech fell into the predicted cell.

The four hypotheses generated by the theory of verbal kinesics all stand the test of empirical investigation. Furthermore, other studies to be reported in future papers dealing with (1) Nixon and Agnew speech performances, (2) the political rhetoric of Robert A. Taft from 1949 until his death in 1953, and (3) Democratic presidential aspirants involved in the 1972 primary contests all confirm the predictive power of the theory of verbal kinesics.

Our goal is eventually to engage in large-scale, cross-linguistic, cross-national elite analysis. However, in terms of American diplomatic history and foreign policy, some new insights are available using the V/H indicators (in addition to the new looks afforded to the Eisenhower through Nixon administrations using paralinguistic indicators). Upon validation of the V/H ratios, spatial symbol scoring was completed for all State of the Union messages of all presidents during the twentieth century.

TABLE 7
VERITCAL AND HORIZONTAL SYMBOL SCORING, STATE OF
THE UNION MESSAGES OF THE TWENTIETH CENTURY

Message by President	V.	H.	V/H	Date	Message by President	V.	H.	V/H	Date
TR					FDR (Continued)				
1	27	7	3.86	12/01	5	1	4	.25	1/38
2	15	1	15.00	12/02	6	4	10	.40	1/39
3	12	3	4.00	12/03	7	4	9	.44	1/40
4	18	4	4.50	12/04	8	3	7	.43	1/41
5	23	6	3.83	12/05	9	3	8	.38	1/42
6	23	5	4.60	12/06	10	4	7	.56	1/43
7	12	3	4.00	12/07	11	4	5	.80	1/44
8	16	3	5.33	12/08	12	11	6	1.83	1/45
WHT					HST				
1	2	1	2.00	12/09	1	15	16	.94	1/46
2	3	0	4.00	12/10	2	4	3	1.33	1/47
3	11	3	3.67	12/11	3	14	19	.74	1/48
4	14	8	1.75	12/12	4	6	14	.43	1/49
					5	10	18	.55	1/50
WW					6	12	19	.63	1/51
1	7	4	1.75	12/13	7	11	27	.41	1/52
2	2	6	.33	12/14	8	18	32	.56	1/53
3	12	13	.92	12/15					
4	0	2	.33	12/16	DDE				
5	9	7	1.29	12/17	1	3	10	.30	1/53
6	6	5	1.20	12/18	2	10	11	.91	1/54
7	3	6	.50	12/19	3	11	11	1.00	1/55
8	2	1	2.00	12/20	4	10	16	.62	1/56
					5	7	10	.70	1/57
WGH					6	10	14	71	1/59
1	14	2	7.00	12/21	7	10	10	1.00	1/59
2	13	5	2.60	12/22	8	11	15	.73	1/60
					9	9	6	1.50	1/61
CC									
1	7	4	1.75	12/23	JFK				
2	7	5	1.40	12/24	1	3	9	.33	1/61
3	11	5	2.20	12/25	2	17	15	1.13	1/62
4	9	2	4.50	12/26	3	8	22	.36	1/63
5	4	2	2.00	12/27					
6	5	1	5.00	12/28	LBJ				
					1	3	4	.75	1/64
HCH					2	8	26	.31	1/65
1	7	1	7.00	12/29	3	6	24	.25	1/66
2	2	7	.29	12/30	4	18	27	.67	1/67
3	4	4	1.00	12/31	5	5	7	.71	1/68
4	4	6	.67	12/32	6	1	12	.08	1/69
FDR					RMN				
1	8	15	.53	1/34	1	4	8	.62	1/70
2	9	13	.69	1/35	2	9	28	.32	1/71
3	4	9	.44	1/36	3	15	13	1.15	1/72
4	3	9	.33	1/37					

The V/H scores, by speech, are given in Table 7. See also Figure 4 for the graph of spatial symbol scores.

Do any historical insights appear in the data presented in these tables? It must again be stressed that the research reviewed here is a more general attempt to develop an international-relations-relevant series of indicators with a general theory of verbal kinesics. As such, we are presenting what Blalock (1969: 151) has called "epistemic correlations," and in spite of the valid urgings of Blalock (1961: 94) and others (Gurr, 1972: 62-63; Palumbo, 1969: 11-12) that one's methodological superego should not be allowed to stand in the way of otherwise "unprovable" findings, the historical findings in this study must be viewed as highly tentative and as only suggestive.

However, given this caveat, let us return to the data. We do see an interesting stress-reduction in Wilson's fifth and sixth State of the Union messages, perhaps commensurate with a reduction in the cognitive dissonance of U.S. neutrality. We likewise see interesting low stress levels in Hoover's third State of the Union message. Only more intense content analysis can ascertain whether or not these shifts are caused in the former case by Wilson's misperception of the necessary extent of American involvement (May, 1959: 425-432) and in the latter case by Hoover's misperception of the extent of the economic crisis (see Warren, 1957).

We see, at least in the State of the Union messages, significant decreases in stress levels for Franklin D. Roosevelt beginning in January 1943, although when "context" is controlled, stress reduction in "foreign" topics only appears in 1945. Of great interest, and further research should be directed at this period, we see relatively low levels of verbal kinesic stress in the "foreign" contexts of Roosevelt's 1938 and 1939 State of the Union messages.

The Eisenhower and Kennedy data has been discussed above. It is interesting to note that Johnson's verbal kinesic stress levels are extremely high in 1965 and 1966, immediately after commiting major resources to Vietnam, and that these stress levels decline until his last State of the Union message (a message given after his policies and party had been soundly repudiated at the polls, and a message that [as he says in the 1969 State of the Union message itself] he almost did not give). In the case of Richard Nixon (in data analyzed to the time of this writing), the only low V/H ratios (high stress— appear in the second State of the Union message, an address given after he and the Republicans had badly "fumbled" the off-year congressional elections (Evans and Novak, 1971: 303-346).

While some of these findings may qualify as "common expectations," others seem to be interesting and worthy of further analysis using

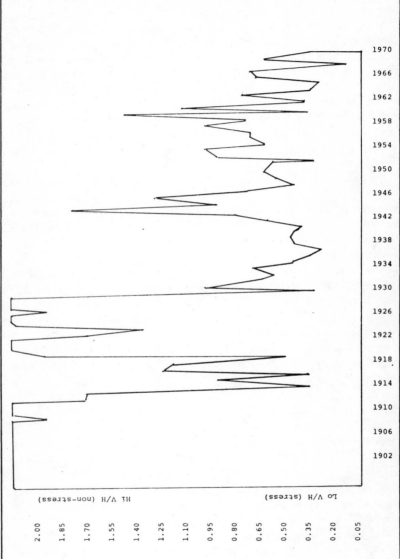

Figure 4: GRAPH OF SPATIAL SYMBOL SCORES, STATE OF THE UNION DATA

multichannel and verbal kinesic indices. As stated above, the actual findings are somewhat supplemental to the development of the technique and the theory of verbal kinesics. As such, they constitute ordinal data that suggest the validity of the theory of verbal kinesics and differential symbolic response in conditions of stress.

NOTES

1. The relationships between communication (words) and behavior (deeds) of political elites have been examined by Margaret Hermann in a fascinating paper presented at the 1972 APSA Convention. However, Hermann does not face the possible problems of lack of equivalency among and between her various indicators. Nevertheless, her study is a landmark venture in this direction of comparing elite words with elite deeds.

2. For example, the lack of mentioning a given subject as an indicator of an unwillingness to talk about or come

3. This assumes that decision-making under stress entails a different cognitive style than decision-making under stress entails a different cognitive style than decision making under nonstress conditions.

4. A cardinal tenet of need-gratification theory is that more primary needs will be satisfied prior to attempting to satisfy the "higher" needs. However, it seems reasonable that such need-gratification is not a mutually exclusive process. Moreover, different individuals probably differentially define success in meeting needs, and the present level of operationalization of these needs does not allow the researcher clearly to identify the need-gratification success (e.g., the spiritual security of martyrs that compels them to reject the satisfaction of the more "primary" physiological needs).

5. For a review of this literature, see Michael Lerner (1969).

6. For example, no less than six different and competing explanations of human motivation are introduced in Erikson's *Young Man Luther* (1958). No attempt is made to sort out or to show the relationships among these theories of motivation.

7. Barber's 1965 study relied heavily on 27 interviews with a mean length of 90 minutes. There is little "actuarial" data, and only an admittedly unrepresentative questionnaire was used to supplement the focused interview technique. Barber's 1972 study relied heavily on secondary source biographies which were "raked through" by Barber's graduate students.

8. A number of those constructs that do retain the greatest amount of empirical support and that do remain as possibly fruitful predictors of elite behavior will be discussed later in this paper.

9. Mischel (1968) gives an in-depth picture of testing conditions and response sets as a major predictor of behavioral response. Atkinson and Litwin (1960) found that different measures of a trait as widely accepted as achievement motivation did not correlate with each other. They conclude: "These results highlight the importance of discovering why different methods of measuring apparently the same human motive do not yield comparable results" (Atkinson and Litwin, 1960: 62).

10. Of course, self-definition may not accurately characterize the self, and such "constructed stabilities" are therefore somewhat limited.

11. Alker's (1972) formulation of situational specificity of response as itself a personality variable (in which he argues that the less "severely disturbed" the individual the greater will be the subject's situational specificity) is a challenging response to and improvement upon Mischel's work. Nevertheless, for most political actors it is assumed here that we are not dealing with "severely disturbed" individuals. This is, of course, a sometimes debatable point.

12. Greenstein is not clear in his arguments as to whether there is one or a limited series of interrelated personality dimensions that have differing levels of "depth" or whether uncorrelated personality dimensions can be "overlaid" upon each other, each with its own level of behavioral activation.

13. Brody notes that McClelland used time-lag methods to show the causal role of motivation to achievement. However, McClelland's cross-national study of achievement used as indicators of the dependent variable the measures of income per capita and kilowatt hours per capita. Brody argues that both of the dependent variables are inherently time-lagged and therefore McClelland's conclusions are somewhat unsubstantiated (pp. 91-93).

14. While no cross-national elite analysis is presented in this paper, the theory from which spatial symbols is drawn powerfully suggests the applicability of this symbol analysis to non-American elites. United States' presidents were selected for a number of reasons (to be explained later), not the least of which was the idiosyncratic role of these presidents in twentieth-century international affairs. In this sense, we must strongly disagree with Rosenau (1966: 45) who argues that the more developed and the more open the political system, the less important are these idiosyncratic variables. There may well be a curvilinear importance to idiosyncratic variables along these two Rosenau independent-variable dimensions, although the bureaucratic and organizational theory needed to support this curvilinearity is beyond the scope of the present paper.

15. While there seems to be a clear behavioral-semantic isomorph in the case of horizontal symbols, the relationship is not so clear in terms of vertical symbols. Three plausible alternatives seem to exist: (1) a cognitive opposite that can be explained in terms of Levi-Strauss' (1963: 89-91) reinterpretation of Radcliffe-Brown's theory of kinship and symbolic totemism; (2) an orienting response in terms of gestalt psychology and place learning; (3) a phylogenetic operant conditioning process in terms of the primate origins of language. While each of these explanations seems possible, no decision at this level of explanation is needed to ascertain the validity of this type of spatial symbol. For a more complete discussion, see Frank (1972).

16. See especially the spatial and body imagery of Jerry Rubin's *Do It!* (1970): "Which do you trust: Richard Milhous Nixon or your own sense organs?" (p. 100); "When you become a nonstudent, sex is better and more plentiful, you smoke more grass, you're healthier and happier and you grow 100 feet tall" (p. 30). It is revealing that Rubin and friends found Che Guevara to be much shorter than they expected him to be (p. 20).

17. A similar isomorph for vertical symbols cannot be constructed until the alternatives discussed in note 17 are fully explored.

18. Eliade's review of territorial symbols and vertical symbols suggests a series of interesting relationships at the symbolic level between authority and nationalism or authority and territoriality. See Ardrey (1967) for the biological and ethological foundations (and functions) of territoriality.

19. Other categories of the Wiener and Mehrabian protocol such as temporal distantiation and complexity of verb structure seem somewhat less warranted than the idea of non-immediacy would suggest, although for their rationale the reader is referred to their 1968 report.

20. Even today the Roman collar of a priest is called a "dog's collar."

21. A recent article by George Mahl (1972) in which he conducted interviews while masking the subjects' ability to hear their own responses (by introducing "white noise" through earphones worn by the subjects) seems to add additional credibility to this three-way interaction.

22. While symptomatic of psychological states, this author knows of no studies on the feedback effect of using such language, e.g., does the use of "distantiated" language reduce the psychic need (or desire) for distantiation?

23. For example, one could treat a symbol as a naturally decaying entity and look at the "half life" of symbolic forms, i.e., when does a symbol lose its "emotional power" and become dated and "camp"?

24. After an extensive review of sources dealing with the diplomatic history of this period, we furthermore concluded as did Kolko and Kolko (1972: 91-95) that the "Russian threat" did not become salient until mid-summer, 1945.

25. This assumption does not invariably hold. When Wilson went to war, making the decision to abandon neutrality seems to have lowered the cognitive dissonance associated with his diplomatic neutrality. Giving in to the wishes of House and of the British, as we shall show later in this paper, actually resulted in a *higher* V/H ratio, thus indicating that at least in this one special case, going to war reduced the tensions associated with neutrality.

26. Dispositional stress is generated over the period of time in which the given president was thinking and writing about the subject area that was perceived to be stressful. Situational stress is a manifestation of actually being in the situation in which you have to verbally communicate what you have previously written. Such stress levels should be similar but not identical.

27. For considerations of using either multiplicative or additive formulas and models, see Singer, Bremer, and Stuckey (1972: 35-36).

28. Here we multiplied (time)/(word length) [speech rate declining as stress increases] by (verbal slips)/(word length) [the relative frequency of verbal slips].

29. We multiplied all verbal slip scores after the illness by a correction factor of the pre- to post-stroke verbal slip ratio.

30. Later in this paper we will discuss the utility of using a multichannel, multi-indicator approach to elite analysis in which linguistic, paralinguistic, and kinesic data are integrated into the research findings. From Table 5 we can see the extent of Kennedy's concern with domestic problems, a point that is not generally recognized, as well as Nixon's concern with "H.E.W. questions" after-fumbling the 1970 off-year elections. Our paralinguistic measure does seem to point out that indeed Kennedy did not realize the inherent problems and dangers involved in U.S. deployment in Southeast Asia.

31. Obviously we are using a process of "creative" (although legitimate) statistics. The obtained scores are similar to the median test described above except that "nonstress" paralinguistic scores need not be inserted into the resulting cells. This omission is justified by the "preconditional" nature of the V/H dispositional stress.

32. Our "P" of the binomial theorem = 68/104 = .65; Q = 1 − P = .35. "P" is established by dividing the total number of verbal (or paralinguistic) stress scores from speech topics above the V/H mean by the total of all paralinguistic stress scores from all speech topic of all analyzed speeches.

REFERENCES

ALKER, H. A. (1972) "Is personality situationally specific or intrapsychically consistent?" J. of Pers. 40, 1: 1-16.

ALLPORT, G. W. (1950) "The role of expectancy," pp. 43-78 in H. Cantril (ed.) Tensions That Cause Wars. Urbana: Univ. of Illinois Press.

ALMOND, G. A. and G. B. POWELL (1966) Comparative Politics: A Developmental Approach. Boston: Little, Brown.

ANDREW, R. J. (1963) "Trends apparent in the evolution of vocalization in the Old World monkeys and apes." Symposium of the Zoological Society of London 10: 89-101.

APTER, D. (1968) "Political religion in the new nations," in D. Apter (ed.) Some Conceptual Approaches to the Study of Modernization. Englewood Cliffs, N.J.: Prentice-Hall. Article originally published in C. Geertz (1963). Old Societies and New Nations. New York: Free Press.

――― (1964) "Introduction: ideology and discontent," in D. Apter (ed.) Ideology and Discontent. New York: Free Press.

ARDREY, R. (1967) The Territorial Imperative. London: Collins.

ATKINSON, J. W. (1957) "Motivational determinants of risk-taking behavior." Psych. Rev. 64: 359-372.

――― and N. T. FEATHER (1966) "Review and appraisal," in J. W. Atkinson and N. T. Feather (eds.) A Theory of Achievement Motivation. New York: John Wiley.

――― and G. H. LITWIN (1960) "Achievement motive and test anxiety conceived as motive to approach success and motive to avoid failure." J. of Ab. and Soc. Psych. 60: 52-63.

BARBER, J. D. (1965) The Lawmakers. New Haven: Yale Univ. Press.

――― (1972) The Presidential Character. Englewood Cliffs, N.J.: Prentice-Hall.

BLALOCK, H. M., Jr. (1969) Theory Construction: From Verbal to Mathematical Formulations. Englewood Cliffs, N.J.: Prentice-Hall.

――― (1961) Causal Inferences in Nonexperimental Research. Chapel Hill: The Univ. of North Carolina Press.

BLAU, P. M. (1964) Exchange and Power in Social Life. New York: John Wiley.

BLOCK, J. and J. BLOCK (1951) "An investigation of the relationship between intolerance of ambiguity and ethnocentrism." J. of Personality 19: 303-311.

BRODY, N. (1972) Personality: Research and Theory. New York: Academic Press.

BRODY, R. A. (1969) "The study of international politics qua science," in K. Knorr and J. N. Rosenau (eds.) Contending Approaches to International Politics. Princeton: Princeton Univ. Press.

BROWN, N. O. (1959) Life Against Death. New York: Random House/Vintage.

BROWN, R. (1965) Social Psychology. New York: Free Press.

――― (1958) Words and Things. New York: Free Press.

――― and E. H. LENEBERG (1954) "A study in language and cognition." J. of Ab. and Soc. Psych. 49: 454-462.

BURNS, J. M. (1970) Roosevelt: Soldier of Freedom. New York: Harcourt-Brace-Jovanovich.

CAMPBELL, J. (1968) The Masks of God: Creative Mythology. New York: Viking.

––– (1949) Hero with a Thousand Faces. Cleveland: World.

CHOMSKY, N. (1968) Language and Mind. New York: Harcourt, Brace, and World.

CHOPLIN, W. D. (1971) Introduction to International Politics. Chicago: Markham.

DARWIN, C. [ed.] (1965) The Expression of the Emotions in Man and Animals. Chicago: Univ. of Chicago Press.

DAVIES, J. C. (1963) Human Nature in Politics. New York: John Wiley.

––– (1962) "Toward a theory of revolution." Amer. Soc. Rev. 27: 5-19.

DeRIVERA, J. (1968) The Psychological Dimensions of Foreign Policy. Columbus, Ohio: Charles E. Merrill.

DeTRACY, D. (1801) Elements d'ideologie as discussed in J. W. Stein (1961) The Mind and the Sword. New York:_____.

DEUTSCH, K. W. (1963) Nerves of Government. New York: Free Press.

––– and L. J. EDINGER (1959) Germany Rejoins the Powers. Stanford: Stanford Univ. Press.

DONLEY, R. E. and D. G. WINTER (1970) "Measuring the motives of public officials at a distance: an exploratory study of American presidents." Behav. Sci. 15: 227-236.

DOUGLAS, M. (1970) Purity and Danger. Baltimore: Penguin.

EASTON, D. (1965) A Systems Analysis of Political Life. New York: John Wiley.

EDINGER, L. J. (1965) Kurt Schumacher: A Study in Personality and Political Behavior. Stanford: Stanford Univ. Press.

EIBL-EIBESFELDT, I. (1970) Ethology: The Biology of Behavior. E. Klinghammer (trans.). New York: Holt, Rinehart and Winston.

EKMAN, P. (1972) Universals and cultural differences in facial expressions of emotion. The Nebraska Symposium on Motivation. Lincoln: Univ. of Nebraska Press.

––– and W. V. FRIESEN (1969) "Constants across cultures in the face and emotion." J. of Pers. and Soc. Psych. 17: 124-129.

––– (1969) "Nonverbal leakage and clues to deception." Psychiatry 32: 88-106.

––– and P. Ellsworth (1972) Emotion in the Human Face. New York: Pergamon.

ELIADE, M. (1969) Cosmos and History. New York: Harper & Row.

––– (1963) Myth and Reality, W. R. Trask. (trans.). New York: Harper & Row.

––– (1960) Myths, Dreams, and Mysteries. P. Mairet (trans.). New York: Harper & Row.

ERIKSON, E. (1969) Gandhi's Truth. New York: W. W. Norton.

––– (1958) Young Man Luther. New York: W. W. Norton.

EVANS, R., Jr. and R. D. NOVAK (1971) Nixon in the White House. New York: Random House.

EYSENCK, H. J. (1967) The Biological Basis of Personality. Springfield, Ill.: Thomas.

––– (1957) The Dynamics of Anxiety and Hysteria. London: Routledge and Kegan Paul.

FARRELL, R. B. [ed.] (1966) Approaches to Comparative and International Politics. Evanston, Ill.: Northwestern Univ. Press.

FEATHER, N. T. (1959) "Subjective probability and decision under uncertainty." Psych. Rev. 66: 150-164.

FINER, H. (1964) Dulles over Suez. London: Heinemann.

FISHER, S. (1970) Body Experience in Fantasy and Behavior. New York: Appleton-Century-Crofts.

――― and S. E. CLEVELAND (1968) Body Image and Personality. 2d rev. ed. New York: Dover.

FRANK, R. S. (1973a) Analysis of nonverbal behavior as a technique for assessing personality at a distance: the McGovern-Humphrey 1972 California Primary debate." To appear in M. G. Hermann and T. W. Milburn (eds.) A Psychological Examination of Political Man. New York: Free Press.

――― (1973b) Biological referents in political rhetoric: a study in verbal kinesics. Paper presented in the IXth World Congress of the International Political Science Association, Montreal, Canada, August 20-25.

――― (1972) Shifts in symbolic communication as a result of international crisis. Ph.D. dissertation. University of Pennsylvania. (unpublished)

FREUD, S. and W. C. BULLITT (1967) Thomas Woodrow Wilson, Twenty-eighth President of the United States: A Psychological Study. Boston: Houghton Mifflin.

GEERTZ, C. [ed.] (1967) "Ritual and Social change," in N. J. Demerath III and R. A. Peterson (eds.) System, Change, and Conflict. New York: Free Press.

――― (1964) "Ideology as a cultural system," in D. Apter (ed.) Ideology and Discontent. New York: Free Press.

――― (1963) Old Societies and New States: The Quest for Modernity in Asia and Africa. New York: Free Press.

GEORGE, A. and J. GEORGE (1964) Woodrow Wilson and Colonel House. New York: John Day.

GLAD, B. (1966) Charles Evans Hughes and the Illusions of Innocency. Urbana: Univ. of Illinois Press.

GOLDMAN-EISLER, F. (1968) Psycholinguistics: Experiments in Spontaneous Speech. New York: Academic Press.

――― (1961) "The distribution of pause durations in speech." Lang. and Speech 4: 232-237.

GREENBERG, J. H. [ed.] (1962) Universals of Language. Cambridge, Mass.: MIT Press.

GREENSTEIN, F. I. (1969) Personality and Politics. Chicago: Markham.

GURR, T. R. (1972) Polimetrics. Englewood Cliffs, N.J.: Prentice-Hall.

――― (1970) Why Men Rebel. Princeton: Princeton Univ. Press.

GUSFIELD, J. R. (1963) Symbolic Crusade. Urbana: Univ. of Illinois Press.

HALLER, W. (1957) The Rise of Puritanism. New York: Harper & Row.

HERMANN, C. (1969) Crises in Foreign Policy. Indianpolis: Bobbs-Merrill.

HERMANN, M. (1972) How leaders process information and the effect on foreign policy. Mershon Center Informal Publications, CREON publication 22 (prepared for delivery at the 1972 Annual Meeting of the American Political Science Association, Washington D.C., September 5-9).

HILGARD, E. R. and G. H. BOWER (1966) Theories of Learning. 3d rev. ed. New York: Appleton-Century-Crofts.

HOLSTI, O. R. (1969) Content Analysis for the Social Sciences and the Humanities. Reading, Mass.: Addison-Wesley.

――― (1965) The 1914 case. Amer. Pol. Sci. REv. 59: 365-378.

――― (1962) "The belief system and national images: a case history." J. of Conflict Res. 6: 244-252.

HYMES, D. (1970) "Linguistic aspects of comparative political research," in R. T. Holt and J. Turner (eds.) The Methodology of Comparative Research. New York: Free Press.

ISRAEL, F. L. [ed.] (1967) The State of the Union Messages. 3 vols. New York: Chelsea House.

JANOS, A. C. (1964) "Authority and violence: the political framework of internal war," in H. Eckstein (ed.) Internal War. New York: Free Press.

JENSEN, L. (1966) "American foreign policy elites and the prediction of international events." Papers, Peace Research Soc. (International): 5: 199-209.

JONAS, H. (1963) The Gnostic Religion. 2d rev. ed. Boston: Beacon.

JONES, J. M. (1955) The Fifteen Weeks. New York: Harcourt, Brace, and World.

KAPLAN, A. (1964) The Conduct of Inquiry. San Francisco: Chandler.

KAPLAN, M. [ed.] (1968) New Approaches to International Relations. New York: St. Martin's Press.

KATZ, E. (1957) "The two-step flow of communication." Pub. Opinion Q. 21: 61-78.

KELMAN, H. C. [ed.] (1965) International Behavior: A Social-psychological Analysis. New York: Holt, Rinehart, and Winston.

KLUCKHOHN, C. (1968) "Recurrent themes in myth and mythmaking," in H. A. Murray (ed.) Myth and Mythmaking. Boston: Beacon.

——— H. A. MURRAY and D. SCHNEIDER (1953) Personality in Nature, Society, and Culture. 2d ed. New York: Alfred A. Knopf.

KNUTSON, J. N. (1972) The Human Basis of the Polity. Chicago: Aldine.

KOLKO, J. and G. KOLKO (1972) The Limits of Power. New York: Harper & Row.

LANE, R. E. (1969) Political Thinking and Consciousness. Chicago: Markham.

LANGER, S. K. (1942) Philosophy in a New Key. New York: New American Library.

LASSWELL, H. D. (1968) "Note on 'types': nuclear, co-relational, and developmental." J. of Soc. Issues 23: 81-91.

——— (1962, original 1948) Power and Personality. New York: Viking.

——— (1960, original 1930) Psychopathology and Politics. New York: Viking Press.

——— (1935) "World politics and personal insecurity," reprinted in (1951) Political Writings of Harold D. Lasswell. Glencoe, Ill.: Free Press.

LAZARUS, R. S. (1966) Psychological Stress and the Coping Process. New York: McGraw-Hill.

LEACH, E. (1969) Claude Levi-Strauss. New York: Viking Press.

——— (1964) "Anthropolitical aspects of language: animal categories and verbal abuses," in E. H. Lenneberg (ed.) New Directions in the Study of Language. Cambridge, Mass.: MIT Press.

LENNEBERG, E. H. (1967) Biological Foundations of Language. New York: John Wiley.

LERNER, D. (1963) "Towards a communication theory of modernization," in L. W. Pye (ed.) Communications and Political Development. Princeton: Princeton Univ. Press.

——— (1958) The Passing of Traditional Society. Glencoe, Ill.: Free Press.

LERNER, M. (1969) "A bibliographical note," in F. I. Greenstein. Personality and Politics. Chicago: Markham.

LEVI-STRAUSS, C. (1969) The Raw and the Cooked. J. Weightman and D. Weightman (trans.). New York: Harper & Row.

——— (1967) Structural Anthropology. C. Jacobson and B. G. Schoepf (trans.). Garden City, N.Y.: Doubleday Anchor.

——— (1967a) "The story of Asdiwal," reprinted in E. Leach (ed.) The Structural Study of Myth and Totemism. London: Tavistock.

——— (1966) The Savage Mind. G. Weidenfeld (trans.). Chicago: Univ. of Chicago Press.

——— (1963) Totemism. R. Needham (trans.). Boston: Beacon.

LIFTON, R. J. (1968) Revolutionary Immortality: Mao Tse-tung and the Chinese Cultural Revolution. New York: Random House.

——— (1967) Boundaries. New York: Random House Vintage.

McCLELLAND, D. C. (1961) The Achieving Society. Princeton: Van Nostrand.

——— J. W. ATKINSON, R. A. CLARK, and E. L. LOWELL (1953) The Achievement Motive. New York: Appleton-Century-Crofts.

MAHL, G. F. (1972) "People talking when they can't hear their voices," in A. W. Siegman and B. Pope (eds.) Studies in Dyadic Communication. New York: Pergamon.

——— (1956) "Measuring the patient's anxiety during interviews from 'expressive' aspects of his speech." Transactions of the New York Academy of Scienc, Series II, 21: 249-257.

MARSH, R. (1971) Agnew the Unexamined Man. New York: M. Evans.

MARSHALL, J. C. (1970) "The biology of communication in man and animals," in J. Lyons (ed.) New Horizons in Linguistics. Baltimore: Penguin.

MASLOW, A. (1954) Motivation and Personality. New York: Harper & Row.

MAY, E. R. (1959) The World War and American Isolation. Chicago: Quadrangle.

MERRITT, R. (1970) Systematic Approaches to Comparative Politics. Chicago: Rand McNally.

——— (1965) "Woodrow Wilson and the 'great and solemn referendum,' 1920." Rev. of Politics 27: 78-104.

MILBURN, T. and M. HERMANN (1974, forthcoming) A Psychological Examination of Political Man.

MILLER, G. A. and D. McNEIL (1969)" Psycholinguistics," in G. Lindzey and E. Aronson (eds.) The Handbook of Social Psychology. 5 Vols. 2d rev. ed. Reading, Mass.: Addison-Wesley, vol. 3.

MISCHEL, W. (1968) Personality and Assessment. New York: John Wiley.

MORTON, J. (1970) Biological and Social Factors in Psycholinguistics. Urbana: Univ. of Illinois Press.

MURRAY, H. A. (1951) "Some basic psychological assumptions and conceptions." Dialectica 5: 266-292.

——— (1938) Explorations in Personality. Oxford: Oxford Univ. Press.

MURRAY, D. C. (1971) "Talk, silence, and anxiety." Psych. Bulletin 65: 244-260.

NORTH, R. C. (1968) "The behavior of nation-states: the problems of conflict and integration," in M. Kaplan (ed.) New Approaches to International Relations. New York: St. Martin's Press.

OGILVIE, D. M. (1969) "Individual and cultural patterns of fantasized flight," in G. Gerber et al., The Analysis of Communication Content. New York: John Wiley.

OSGOOD, C. (1957) The Measurement of Meaning. Urbana: Univ. of-Illinois Press.

PALUMBO, D. J. (1969) Statistics-in Political and Behavioral Science. New York: Appleton-Century-Crofts.

PIAGET, J. (1971) Biology and knowledge, an essay on the relations between organic regulations and cognitive processes, B. Walsh (trans.). Chicago: Univ. of Chicago Press.

POOL, I. de SOLA (1970) The Prestige Press: A Comparative Study of Political Symbols. Cambridge, Mass.: MIT Press.

——— (1963) "The mass media and politics in the modernization process," in L. W. Pye (ed.) Communications and Political Development. Princeton: Princeton Univ. Press.

POSTMAN, L. (1961) "The present status of interference theory," in C. N. Cofer (ed.) Verbal Learning and Verbal Behavior. New York: McGraw-Hill.

PRIBRAM, K. H. (1971) Languages of the Brain, Experimental Paradoxes and Principles of Neuropsychology. Englewood Cliffs, N.J.: Prentice-Hall.

PRZEWORSKI, A. and H. TEUNE (1970) The Logic of Comparative Social Inquiry. New York: John Wiley.

PYE, L. W. (1963) "Introduction," in L. W. Pye (ed.) Communications and Political Development. Princeton: Princeton Univ. Press.

RANK, O. (1959) [ed.] The Myth of the Birth of the Hero and Other Writings. F. Robbins and S. E. Jelliffe (trans.). New York: Random House.

RENSHON, S. (1972) The psychological origins of political efficacy: the need for personal control. Ph.D. dissertation. University of Pennsylvania. (unpublished)

ROGOW, A. (1963) James Forrestal: A Study of Personality, Politics, and Policy. New York: Macmillan.

ROKEACH, M. (1960) The Open and Closed Mind. New York: Basic Books.

ROSENAU, J. N. (1966) "Pre-theories and theories of foreign policy," in R. B. Farrell (ed.) Approaches to Comparative and International Politics. Evanston, Ill.: Northwestern Univ. Press.

RUBIN, J. (1970) Do It! New York: Simon and Schuster.

SCHWARTZ, D. C. (1972) Talk presented to the Yale University Psychology and Politics seminar.

——— (1970) "A theory of revolutionary behavior," in J. C. Davies (ed.) When Men Rebel and Why. New York: Free Press.

SIEGEL, S. (1956) Nonparametric Statistics for the Behavioral Sciences. New York: McGraw-Hill.

SINGER, J. D. (1968) "The incompleat theorist," in K. Knorr and J. N. Rosenau (eds.) Contending Approaches to International Politics. Princeton: Princeton Univ. Press.

——— (1968a) Man and world politics: the psycho-cultural interface. J. of Soc. Issues 24: 127-156.

——— [ed.] (1965) Human Behavior and International Politics: Contributions from the Social-Psychological Sciences. Chicago: Rand McNally.

——— (1961) "The level-of-analysis problem in international relations," in K. Knorr and S. Verba (eds.) The International System: Theoretical Essays. Princeton: Princeton Univ. Press.

——— S. BREMER, and J. STUCKEY (1972) "Capability distribution, uncertainty, and major power war, 1820-1965," in B. M. Russett (ed.) Peace, War, and Numbers. Beverly Hills: Sage.

SMELSER, N. (1962) Theory of Collective Behavior. New York: Free Press.

SMITH, M. B. (1968) "A map for the analysis of personality and politics." J. of Soc. Issues 24: 15-28.

SNYDER, R. C. (1961) International relations theory—continued. World Politics 13: 300-312.

——— H. W. BRUCK; and B. M. SAPIN [eds.] (1962) Foreign Policy Decision-making: An Approach to the Study of International Politics. New York: Free Press.

STEIN, J. W. (1961) The Mind and the Sword. New York: Twayne.

STONE, P. J. (1969) "Confrontation of issues: excerpts from the discussion session at the conference," in G. Gerbner et al., The Analysis of Communication Content. New York: John Wiley.

SULLIVAN, M. P. (1972) "Symbolic involvement as a correlate of escalation: the Vietnam case," in B. M. Russett (ed.) Peace, War, and Numbers. Beverly Hills: Sage.

TOLMAN, E. C. (1955) Principles of performance. Psych. Rev. 62: 315-326.

––– (1951) Behavior and Psychological Man: Essays in Motivation and Learning. Berkely: Univ. of California Press.

TUKEY, J. W. (1970) Exploratory Data Analysis, limited prelim. ed. Reading, Mass.: Addison-Wesley.

TURNER, V. (1969) The Ritual Process. Chicago: Aldine.

VERBA, S. (1961) Assumptions of rationality and non-rationality in models of the international system. World Politics 24.

WALZER, M. (1968) The Revolution of the Saints. New York: Atheneum.

WARREN, H. G. (1967) Herbert Hoover and ˏthe Great Depression. New York: Norton.

WHORF, B. L. (1956) Language, Thought, and Reality. Cambridge, Mass.: MIT Press.

WIENER, M. and A. MEHRABIAN (1968) Language Within Language. New York: Appleton-Century-Crofts.

––– S. DeVOE, S. RUBINOW, and J. GELLER (1972) Nonverbal behavior and nonverbal communication. Psych. Rev. 79: 185-214.

WILKINSON, D. O. (1969) Comparative Foreign Relations: Framework and Methods. Encino, Calif.: Dickenson.

WILLS, G. (1969) Nixon Agonistes. New York: New American Library.

WITKIN, H. A. et al. (1962) Psychological Differentiation. New York: John Wiley.

ZINNES, D. A. (1968) "The expression and perception of hostility in prewar crisis: 1914," in J. D. Singer (ed.) Quantitative International Politics. New York: Free Press.

ZIPF, G. K. (1949) Human Behavior and the Principle of Least Effort. Reading, Mass.: Addison-Wesley.

––– (1935) The Psycho-Biology of Language. Boston: Houghton Mifflin.

REVISED CODING RULES FOR SPATIAL SYMBOLS, NON-IMMEDIACY, AND BODY IMAGERY

VERTICAL SYMBOLS

1. You are looking for "symbolic" references. Except for sentences with multiple clauses, each with different symbolic components, there generally will be only one "symbol set" per sentence.

    (a) "Industry is rising and the farmers stand tall." (Code twice)

    (b) "Let us build our influence and our trade potential." (Code once)

2. Determining symbolic usage:

    (a) Look first for metaphor, i.e., the replacement of a common word (or phrase) with a not-so-common word (or phrase) or with an "elaboration" of a common word.

    (b) Do not code "rising taxes," "rising production," "rising tariffs," etc. In other words, do not code statistical and/or production "rises." You can code for major social-ecnomic forces, but not for specific subgroups.

    "Industry is rising." (Code)

    "The steel monopolies are rising." (Do not code)

3. Do not code for ambiguous directional reference. Do not code for 'spreading', do not code for 'strengthening', do not code for "growing strong" (here "growing" means "becoming").

4. You should also code for positive vertical "presence" (see 9 below) and for vertical situation. Even if there is no movement going on here. Code for "standing," "standing tall," "aspire to a high place," "highest expression of" "our success is a temple to our achievements," etc.

5. You can code for denials such as "We have refused to join the League not out of aloofness but out of conviction."

6. If defined vertically, you can code foreign entities, friends or enemies.

    (a) "Let's build the security of our allies." (Code)

    (b) "Our enemies stand unmasked as outlaws." (Code)

    (c) "Let's help the Chinese rise from poverty." (Code)

    (d) "We face a growing threat." (Do not code)

7. "Grow," in vertical symbolism, much like "progress" in horizontal symbolism, can only rarely be coded, and then only when context is highly sumbolic. Code: "We grow under law," "we grow in wisdom with each passing day."

8. You must code for vertically relational symbols. Code for "roots" and for "foundations," (but do not code for the verb "founding") and for "base" if used in a symbolic sense, e.g., "At the base of our prosperity lies our freedom." Code references to things above and below if they are positively valued.

   (a) "Our country was built upon freedom." (Code)

   (b) "Above all else lies our sacred duty." (Code)

   (c) "We have government under law." (Code)

   (d) "Above all else, remember me." (Do not code)

   (e) "Heavy duties weigh upon us." (Do not code)

9. Do not code for burdens, decaying, "breaking down," etc.

HORIZONTAL SYMBOLS

1. You are coding for symbolism, and except in the case of two distinct clauses (e.g., "Let the word go forth that the torch has been passed"), there generally will be only one "symbol set" per sentence.

2. Determining symbolic usage:

   (a) Look first for metaphor, i.e., the replacement or "elaboration" of a common word with a not-so-common word or phrase.

      "We must understand the path of foreign policy." (Code)

      "We must understand the changes in foreign policy." (Do not code)

      "Let's explore Alaska." (Do not code)

      "Let's explore our differences." (Code)

   (b) A word by itself, no matter how seemingly horizontal, is not symbolic unless the referent is symbolic, i.e., the referent generally is not used with the horizontal word. In other words, it is normal to explore Alaska, but normally we discuss, not explore, our differences.

   (c) Code for politically central referents or their equivalents. Code for: "the nation," "our people," "peace," "new world," etc. As equivalents code for: "let us advance our purpose," "let the word go forth," etc.

   (d) Do not code for taxes, specific alliances, full income, higher tariffs, etc. (See 2b, Vertical Symbols)

   (e) Do not code for non-collective referents. "We must help those left out to catch up." (Do not code)

3. Be very careful of references to time and to progress. You can code "beginning anew," "we stand before a new era," etc. You cannot code for "the swift flow of events" (reality is swirling around us or we are being passively carried along; in neither case is this the symbolism of a conscious, "heroic" journey). Almost never code "progress" unless the referent is very symbolic. Do not code "economic progress," "the talks are progressing well," "we have made progress in the war," etc.

4. Code for what a traveller generally does. Code "Let us chart our goals." But do not code for goal attained or nearly attained symbols. Do not code "stop(s)."

   (a) "We have taken steps in this direction." (Do not code)

   (b) "Step by step we shall move forward together." (Code only once for "move forward together")

   (c) "Soon we shall attain our goals." (Do not code)

   (d) "Let us chart our goals." (Code)

   (e) "We have gone far enough." (Do not code)

   (f) "We have gone too fast." (Code)

5. Only code for unidirectional movement. Do not code for "called," "summoned," "brought together," "join together."

6. Do not code for simple change. "The world will look different to our children." (People can remain still and the seasons may change around them.) But you can code for "standing before a new age," if the context refers to moving into that new age.

   (a) "In the period that lies ahead. . . . " (Code)

   (b) "Let us consider the past, the present, and the future." (Do not code)

   (c) "Let us neither despair of the future nor indict the past." (Do not code)

7. "New directions open up." (Do not code) Movement has not begun or even been called for.

8. Be very alert and do code for implicit symbolism:

   (a) "Peace is more than a haven for the weary." (Code)

   (b) "We are groping for a new solution." (Code)

   (c) "We are seeking a wider peace." (Code)

   (d) "We are seeking to establish a better world." (Do not code) "Seeking" plus "to" is the equivalent of attempting, a nonhorizontal symbol.

   (e) "We are embarking on a new decade." (Code)

NON-IMMEDIACY SCORING

The general goal of non-immediacy analysis is to try to ascertain the "distance" the individual places between himself and the topic about which he is talking.

1. Spatial Category: Code for non-immediacy when the speaker uses demonstratives such as "that" and "those" in a context where "the," "this," or "these" would be sufficient.

   "I don't agree with "that" type of person." (Code with "S")

   "I don't agree with "this" type of person." (Do not code)

Exception to spatial category: do not code where reference is made to the normal past.

"At that time, 1945, it seemed a good thing to do." (Do not code)

2. Temporal category: Code for non-immediacy when unnecessarily complex verb forms are used. Use this rule fairly strictly.

"We will find a way." (Do not code)

"We will be finding a way." (Code with "T")

"I should like to call your attention" (Code with "T")

"I wish to call your attention" (Do not code)

3. Denotative Specificity Category: This is a general category coded for non-immediacy in which in answer to a question, the answer avoids directly answering the question.

Question: "Do you think our policy in Vietnam is hurting the country's economy?"

Answer: "There are really many things that endanger the nation's economic health; Vietnam is but one of them." (Code with "DS")

4. Negation Category: Code for non-immediacy where opposite attribute is used with a negation.

"Our policy is not a bad one." (Code with "N")

"Our policy is a good one." (Do not code)

5. Objective Pronoun Category: Code for the use of objective pronouns to denote speaker or speaker's group.

"Their policies interest me." (Code with "OP")

"I'm interested in their policies." (Do not code)

6. Passive Category: Code only when subject is "self" or speaker's own group.

"I was brainwashed by the generals." (Code with "P")

"They were outmanouvered." (Do not code)

"We were defeated." (Code with "P")

"We lost." (Do not code)

7. Class Category: Code the generalization to a group for which the specific is more appropriate.

"One would say their policies are suspect." (Code with "C")

"I would say their policies are suspect." (Do not code)

"You'd think he should succeed." (Code with "C")

"I would think he should succeed." (Do not code)

8. Modification Category: Code for non-immediacy when a qualification is introduced into the verbalization.

"It is probably true that we will win." (Code with "M")

"We will win." (Do not code)

"Obviously, Vietnamization will work." (Code with "M")

"I find their policies destructive." (Code with "M")

"Their policies are destructive." (Do not code)

9. Multiple Coding: It is possible to code for non-immediacy twice in the same sentence.

BODY IMAGE DICTIONARY

Coding Rules: The coding unit is the word or phrase. Two coding references conceivably can be found in the same sentence.

Category 1: Code for all references to bodily parts that human being have, whether reference is explicitly to human body part or not.

Category 2: Code for references to animals, animallike characteristics, and parts of animals.

Category 3: Code for health or sickness.

Category 4: Code for references to disease, filth, dirty, decay, disorder.

Category 5: Code for purity, cleanliness.

Category 6: Code for all references to receptacles and containers. This includes general references to "the body" (The body politic of America. . . .).

Category 7: Code all references for any type of body whose "boundaries" are crossed, either penetrating the boundary or if something is flowing out across the boundaries. Nota bene: Penetration and emission scores need not explicitly refer to bodily parts in the organic sense. (Like a volcano, violence erupted in the streets.)

Category 8: Code for any verb structure that implies explicit bodily functioning (eating, drinking, bathing, sleeping, etc.). Do not code for simple physical movement such as running, moving, travelling, etc.

Category 9: Code for all chronological stages in the life cycle. The following concepts are acceptable: birth, rebirth, infancy (infant), childhood (child), youth (young), adolescence (adolescent), maturity (mature), senility (senile), death (dying). Code only if these are attributes not directly defining people or groups. Do not code "The youth of America have no patriotism." Code "This county is no longer in its youth." Do not code, "old," as it has too many nonbody image references.

Category 10: Code for references, either explicit or implicit, to arousal ("America cannot live on adrenalin alone"). Also code for references to extreme emotions to which human bodies often react (e.g., "pain," "painful") or which often result in the response of overt human movement ("I was ecstatic when I heard the news").

ROBERT S. FRANK received his Ph.D. in International Relations from the University of Pennsylvania. He has completed post-doctoral training at Yale University in the Psychology and Politics program supported by the National Institute of Mental Health. Dr. Frank is currently a Research Associate at the Foreign Policy Research Institute and Research Coordinator of the Political Communications Research Group at the FPRI. He has published articles in Journalism Quarterly *and the* Experimental Study of Politics *and is the author of* Message Dimensions of Television News. *His article, "Non-textual Psychopolitical Assessment: A Multimethod Approach to Elite Analysis," will appear in Margaret G. Hermann and Thomas Milburn's* A Psychological Assessment of Political Man.

A Better Way of Getting New Information

Research, survey and policy studies that say what needs to be said—no more, no less.

The Sage Papers Program

Eight regularly-issued original paperback series that bring, at an unusually low cost, the timely writings and findings of the international scholarly community. Since the material is updated on a continuing basis, each series rapidly becomes a unique repository of vital information.

Authoritative, and frequently seminal, works that NEED to be available

- To scholars and practitioners
- In university and institutional libraries
- In departmental collections
- For classroom adoption

Sage Professional Papers

COMPARATIVE POLITICS SERIES

INTERNATIONAL STUDIES SERIES

ADMINISTRATIVE AND POLICY STUDIES SERIES

AMERICAN POLITICS SERIES

CONTEMPORARY POLITICAL SOCIOLOGY SERIES

POLITICAL ECONOMY SERIES

Sage Policy Papers

THE WASHINGTON PAPERS

Sage Research Papers

SAGE PUBLICATIONS
The Publishers of Professional Social Science
Beverly Hills • London

Sage Professional Papers in Comparative Politics

Editors: **Aristide R. Zolberg,** *University of Chicago*
Richard Merritt, *University of Illinois*

(Volumes I thru IV edited by Harry Eckstein
and Ted Robert Gurr)

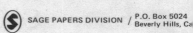

SAGE PAPERS DIVISION / P.O. Box 5024
Beverly Hills, Ca

PROFESSIONAL PAPER **SUBSCRIPTION** INFORMATION APPEARS ELSEWHERE ON THIS